P9-DNN-700

Hildegard, the Last Year

Hildegard, the Last Year

Barbara Lachman

Shambhala
Boston & London
1997

Shambhala Publications, Inc.
Horticultural Hall
300 Massachusetts Avenue
Boston, MA 02115
http://www.shambhala.com

© 1997 by Barbara Lachman

All rights reserved. No part of this book may be reproduced in any form or by any means, electronic or mechanical, including photocopying, recording, or by any information storage and retrieval system, without permission in writing from the publisher.

9 8 7 6 5 4 3 2 1

First Edition

Printed in the United States of America
♾ This edition is printed on acid-free paper that meets the American National Standards Institute Z39.48 Standard.

Distributed in the United States by Random House, Inc., and in Canada by Random House of Canada Ltd

Library of Congress Cataloging-in-Publication Data

Lachman, Barbara.
Hildegard, the last year/Barbara Lachman.
p. cm.
ISBN 1-57062-315-5
1. Hildegard, Saint, 1098–1179—Fiction. 2. Civilization, Medieval—12th century—Fiction. 3. Christian women saints—Germany—Fiction. 4. Germany—History—843–1273—Fiction. 5. Women mystics—Germany—Fiction. I. Title.
PS3562.A244H5 1997 97-7506
813′.54—dc21 CIP

To my first reader and
beloved *symmysta,* John.

Contents

Acknowledgments

Every work of historical reconstruction must depend upon the work of first-rate scholars. Now that the name of Hildegard of Bingen has suddenly become nearly a catchall for New Age generalizations, the pioneering work of Peter Dronke in England, Barbara Newman in this country, and Sabina Flanagan in Australia, not to speak of Benedictine nuns such as Anna Silvas, Adelgundis Führkötter, Pudentiana Barth, and M. Immaculata Ritscher, is more important than ever. My thanks for their dedicated labors.

As well, I am grateful to have had the rare opportunity to live among, catalogue, and exhibit with John Blackley the extraordinary collection of books at La Casa del Libro in San Juan, Puerto Rico. Those four years awakened a great curiosity about and appreciation for the making of books and manuscripts and the workings of medieval monastic scriptoria. And I am grateful for the abiding presence of music over a fairly long life.

Finally, I give thanks to the colleagues with whom I work, family, and friends, for their help and for tolerating the fact that my mind is increasingly occupied in other times and places; and to my editor, Peter Turner, and agent, Howard Sandum, for their encouragement and guidance.

Introduction

After nine hundred years, Hildegard's creative life is more puzzling than ever; her accomplishments make her an anomaly. We know she was born in the year 1098, the tenth child to a family of noble birth in the Rhineland, and that at the age of eight she was given by her own parents into the care of a woman named Jutta, also of gentle birth, who lived as an anchoress within the walls of a men's monastery named after St. Disibode. But what could that have meant? Those of us who live with Hildegard as a kind of icon press for greater understanding of her. Dozens of scholarly articles speculate on the basis of ferreted records and Latin manuscripts, common sense and educated guesses.

What would "educated" mean to Hildegard, she who once wrote that she composed chant even though she had never studied music, and whose only teacher was the untaught Jutta? By the time she was a young woman, she was part of a small group, still living at St. Disibode's, all nuns professed according to the Rule of St. Benedict. This means she knew entirely by heart all the Latin texts and music for the Mass Propers and the seven daily offices of psalmody, plus all the chants for Matins, the great night office with lessons and responsories. Yet the question of her learning tugs at the imagination.

Very late in her long life—for she lived nearly eighty-one years—in an autobiographical fragment that was part of her earliest biography, Hildegard talks about the course of her visionary life: not even from earliest childhood, but from the time she was in her mother's womb, God had implanted this capacity. Attempts she made to inquire how she could see such strange things with her inner eyes in the clear light of day were misunderstood, so for a long time she concealed the experience. When she was finally driven to talk about the visions more explicitly, it was to Jutta, who could not help her understand them and left her more puzzled than ever, fearful of the learned, worldly men who might have answers but might also laugh or condemn her for what was not ordinary behavior in a woman. She was very often ill, with mysterious and sometimes paralyzing symptoms. By the time Hildegard began inquiring into her visions, first with Jutta and then with the monk Volmar, the visions had taken on an admonitory, even didactic, quality. They were strongly visual, with precise forms and colors, but had the added feature of a voice—the voice of the Old Testament female figure Sapientia, or Wisdom, who interpreted every burning figure in detail.

Yet women were to keep silence and were forbidden to teach, and we know that Hildegard was in her forties by the time she was able to overcome her terrors sufficiently to dictate any of the visions to Volmar and then make an appeal for their approval. She wrote to the powerful, influential Cistercian Bernard of Clairvaux; consequently her writings were examined by a synod of bishops and, under the ægis of Pope Eugenius III, given approbation as embodying the gift of prophecy. Thus it was accepted that, like the Old Testament prophets, Hildegard could discern through her visions the very deepest meanings in what might appear to others to be mere ordinary experience. Within the ten years required for Hildegard to finish dictating the *Scivias* visions to Volmar, she had begun to receive a staggering number of letters seeking her prophetic advice about a multiplicity of subjects both human and religious.

Even Hildegard herself knew by this time that she was a mouthpiece for the Divine. But then she received a powerful vision that concerned the direction of her own life and that of the small group of nuns whom she had shepherded since Jutta's death: she was to leave the confines of the male monastery and establish physically an autonomous community, an independent entity. The monks at St. Disibode's, led by their abbot Kuno, opposed the move absolutely. It was unthinkable; besides, the presence of Hildegard the prophetess in their midst by this time brought favor to their house.

Hildegard was not to be dissuaded from the vision for her women; it only grew stronger with time, as did the opposition of Abbot Kuno. The mysterious, paralyzing illness recurred, lovingly attended by a young nun, Rikkarda; the vision was encouraged by the loyal Volmar. Finally, Abbot Kuno observed the extent of Hildegard's illness with his own eyes and understood that only if he acceded to her vision could she possibly recover health. Through Rikkarda's mother, Hildegard acquired land at an abandoned shrine to St. Rupert, and the twenty or so women set out to form their own convent.

Practical problems proliferated. The dowries of her women needed transferring; she needed a priest for Mass and (no small thing) a secretary for the constant flowering of the prophetic voice within. Remarkably, she managed to win the dowries and Volmar, against Kuno's wishes.

She flourished. As the *magistra* of her own community, it was she who taught all the music for the Divine Office; and we find that, within the first decade at St. Rupertsberg, she had composed and written down texts and music for antiphons, responsories, hymns, and sequences, plus the first extant sung morality play, based on a struggle pitting the devil against sixteen distinct female Virtues and their queen. She also produced during this time a complete herbal and a treatise on the causes and cures of a variety of illnesses.

All this in spite of what she saw as a betrayal in the early years of the new community, when her beloved nun Rikkarda was summarily called to become abbess of a Benedictine house in the extreme north of Germany, a move arranged by Rikkarda's brother, the archbishop of Bremen. This time Hildegard did not prevail, despite the nuns' vow of stability and in spite of letters to Rikkarda's brother and mother, to the archbishop of Mainz, and to the pope himself. The young nun was fetched by the authorities and taken to preside at Bremen, only to die suddenly and inexplicably within a year.

Still Hildegard continued to create. With Volmar's help there were more books of visions and an ever growing body of letters. One correspondent was Emperor Frederick Barbarossa, who granted protective immunity to St. Rupertsberg. She founded a daughter house across the Rhine in Eibingen and—in spite of proscriptions against women teachers—made preaching tours that took her far from home, denouncing as a prophet the multitude of abuses she saw proliferating among the clergy, within monastic communities, and in worldly individual hearts.

Not that her health was ever robust. Time and time again she would exhaust herself and reexperience the mysterious illness, and then she would recover, driven in part by the need to speak out in times she knew to be worsening. The German emperor Barbarossa three times supported if not set up antipopes to oppose the lawfully elected Alexander III—first Victor, then Paschal, followed by Callistus. Through it all, Hildegard stood fearlessly behind Alexander and castigated Barbarossa for his machinations. Barbarossa involved himself further in religious administration: by the time Hildegard reached old age, she saw Christian of Buch, brilliant linguist and politician, appointed archbishop of her own diocese of Mainz, while he in fact waged political battles for imperial lands and power in Italy. She could not have known that this powerful prelate would directly oppose her in her last year.

Hildegard produced her final and by far most original book of visions in 1173. As she was finishing the monumental work, known as *Liber divinorum operum,* or simply *De operatione dei,* her devoted scribe Volmar died and, as she said with great poignancy, left her as an orphan. She who was given away by her parents at age eight, who renounced the world with Benedictine vows, who felt betrayed by a spiritual daughter and by an emperor she had counseled, was orphaned finally and only in her eighth decade by the death of the companion of her long creative life. Now she had to stand against a force of silence that threatened to take away the life's breath of her community, its sung chant—and have the courage to understand and go to meet her own approaching death.

Part One

July 22, 1177
Feast of St. Mary Magdalene

Three goldfinches in the chicory darted out this morning on my supported walk. Glints of yellow-green flashing among the blue rays teased me without mercy for my shuffle. I seem to sink ever deeper into the ground. Ankles gone, knees next. At my death they'll first need to pull me from the earth that draws me nesting, before they can carry me to my grave in the orchard.

How we are all dazzled by the movement of wings in the air—the stabbing color of these finches, the assured circling of the hawk, the strength of the eagle poised for prey. *Exsultet jam angelica turba caelorum.*[1] Angels rejoice in heaven, the celestial birds of our deep belief.

All these images of the air are such youthful experience. Companions to sun, dancers with stars are innocent of living, of suffering. So little they know of mature experience, of aging in appreciation. Our holy martyrs, to whom we bow in admiration, were nearly all by definition slaughtered in a state of innocence, as was their great exemplar Jesus Christ, barely entered his fourth decade. Who among our army of saints did not suffer untimely death? When Becket was so brutally murdered, the entire Christian world shook, as he was cut down at the very beginning of a courageous portrayal of newfound religious conviction. The news of my daughter Rikkarda's untimely death was pierced agony.

We know so little of aging in faith, and of its virtues. The Blessed Virgin perhaps, but she remains so wordless before us, more narration than true experience. Excepting weight. That we can understand. We can see the weight of sorrow in her body at the foot of the cross, see her taking his weight at the deposition and preparation for burial, see her yet remaining available to more responsibility with the searing of Pentecost and the demands of an expectant, evangelizing flock. Yet she remains mute, and we have only a dull sense of the weight of her experience for witness.

Often I feel like a weighted pioneer of old age: I report a pilgrimage not to an honored sacred shrine, but to a place of unexplored mystery. My chief companion is still Volmar, though he died to the world some three years ago and was never aware of growing in age as I am. Certainly it is a pilgrimage not in the elements of air and water, but into those of earth and fire. If I still receive new music, its tempo is slower, its movement more deliberate, with a deep joy unheard in youth. Its colors are darker, more intense, minerals burnished by fire. Its rhythm has less to do with the flight of birds and hovering of angels than with long, slow death-preparation and the seasonal rebirth of deciduous trees.

August 15, 1177
Feast of the Assumption of the Virgin

News has been brought that negotiations in Venice were concluded successfully last month, and the long schism that rent the Church for eighteen years is ended. Alexander is finally acknowledged by the universal Church as the true pope; the energetic maneuverings of not one, but three successive antipopes have failed at last to unseat him. They say Frederick Barbarossa recommended that the third pretender be granted an abbey, to which he would return as leader. The thought that he should serve as abbot to a community of religious is devastating.[2]

One dares wonder anew at the state of the soul of our emperor. His kingship was celebrated almost simultaneously with the consecration of our cloister church here at Rupertsberg in 1152, when we were no more than a fledgling nest of women; our correspondence began about the same time. Hopeful beginnings acknowledged and exchanged personally between us were followed shortly by his elevation to emperor. But while we at Rupertsberg struggled to follow a vision directed by the Voice of Wisdom, the emperor's path has not been true. Again and again he has thrown his power unjustly to the support of that which could only fragment the Church while elevating the empire and himself. I cautioned him to curb his overblown ambition, at one point even informing him how he had appeared to me in a vision as a stupid infant and a madman.[3]

But he would not be halted, and managed to secure

a strange following; even some monastics were not strong enough to maintain loyalty to the legitimacy of Pope Alexander. I know that poor Elisabeth of Schönau mistakenly supported Frederick's illegitimate choices up to the time of her death.

It tires me just to think of trying again to unravel the political intrigues that might lie behind Emperor Frederick's actions, to say nothing of the negligence of our own clergy. Yet I must clearly discern evil if I am to speak against it and counsel my women against its contagion. I remember that, while Cologne seethed with a growing number of heretical Cathars, Rainald, then archbishop—another of Barbarossa's chancellors—was otherwise occupied with imperial business, neglecting his legitimate duties in that noble city, where the Church was floundering without any real spiritual discipline. Already this was too clear when I visited the holy resting place of St. Ursula, saw with my own eyes her ancient church and relics; but there was too little time for contemplation when my energy had to be committed to speaking out publicly against abuses. A few loyal prelates, such as Philip the cathedral's deacon, honestly listened and continued to meditate on the message I had delivered, writing to seek more direction from me; but most in the city were abandoned to further intrigue.

By the time of Paschal's death, in fact, it should hardly have surprised anyone that our ambitious Frederick Barbarossa was willing to recognize yet another antipope rather than persevere in difficult negotiations. So antipope Callistus was pawn for a decade, with little positive role except to further the shame of the state of our Church and block the lawful going forward of Pope Alexander. Thank God it is over, and that I have lived to see a reconciliation long overdue.

No thanks to the emperor, whose soul is by this time murky with sin and who never responded to the God-given signs and warnings I communicated to him, even when I knew his continued wrongdoings threatened his life as imperial leader. It must be ten years since I told him how God's wrath had been revealed to me:

> He Who Is said, "I annihilate prideful disobedience, and I
> myself obliterate the opposition of those who despise me.
> Woe, woe to the evil enemies who spurn me! Hear this,
> king, if you wish to live—else my sword will strike you down."[4]

The times we live in count loyalty as nothing, whether loyalty to men lawfully chosen with the blessing of God or loyalty to God and His commandments. There is no discernment of a difference between the willful imposition of one's own ambition and the will of God.

I have long since given up the public speaking tours I made for a decade in the '60s, which were always followed by collapse, illness, exhaustion, and (Mother of God help me) discouragement at the impossibility of being heard in a Church still torn and emasculated by this division of its primary office.

I am finished with the world. I must be at peace in the Word on earth.

August 17, 1177
Octave of St. Lawrence, Martyr

The Te Deum was beautiful at the end of Matins yesterday, sung in thanks for peace in the whole Church. I have too often been lacking in patience with their voices; truth is, they do justice to any of the music I have required of them. Given time and dailiness, they have not failed to praise God in song, even when I myself was not satisfied. It wasn't until I had visited a number of other Benedictine communities that I began to hear my own choir without punishing expectations.

When all my women gather for more solemn festival praises, it is yet another species of sound, for subtle differences grow separately in our house across the Rhine in Eibingen. I hear it in the singing of that daughter house, taste it in the food, and see it in the light their building encloses. Even though my twice-weekly crossings are progressively more difficult and may soon be reduced to once each week, I enjoy observing the differences. I love the ritual of the crossing itself.

They nearly carry me down the steep bank these days to the barge that ferries me across. Their hands are remarkably strong, and they are so carefully silent—no grunting or sounds of effort over the rutted terrain. I pretend not to notice they are propelling me to the boat. I dictate orders, sometimes brief messages for a scribe, so the routine continues like well-lubricated wheels. I continue to give directions as leather thongs secure me to my seat. My bones are too brittle for a fall on the planking, and without warning my joints sometimes fail to connect these days.

The smell of the river is wonderful, both briny and of the earth that beds it. Young fish often wriggle into our path; plants color the ragged banks. Its colors are always changing, brown and turgid like old stirred soup if rains have churned it, clearer and more blue under placid skies.

Time was I made the trip almost daily, as we were first setting up the daughter house in Eibingen. Daily and often with Volmar, directly after Mass, I was so eager to see progress and quicken necessary decisions. I also remember standing firmly aboard without him, even on stormy days feeling the river-swells directly through my feet.

By that time the ways of the river were friendly to me. As with so many things I know, I first learned the river's length as a pilgrim, but with the intention more to teach than to learn. The routes of my preaching tours were governed by the way the rivers flow out like branches from the mighty trunk of the Rhine itself, which carries travelers in one direction to Cologne, in the other to Mainz. Other times the same Rhine carried me to the branch that is the Moselle leading to Trier and Metz. The last tour was the longest, and for that we traveled the Rhine east to the Main, all the way to Würzburg and Bamberg. Up and down, north and south, climbing on this great tree of a river, and on to its contributing rivers. It was as if the Rhine led us through a vast bloodworks feeding a body of monasteries and cathedrals, and I always returning at last, exhausted, to the beauty of the valley of the Nahe, our own vein of the Rhine, with its welcoming Sponheim castle and luxurious green hills covered with vineyards.

The first impressions from this watery length were of endless vistas. What I had loved from Bingen was multiplied, extended by the surprising shifts in course, the sight of a cross or tower on a distant hill, the sound of familiar but slightly differently pitched bells from a distance, everywhere the grandeur of God's space. All I had viewed in the distance from our mountain above, I saw anew and enlarged—sharp geometry of tended vines, rounded forests of evergreens, and clouds of tiny waterbirds feeding. From below, on the river, tall hills topped with bold constructions of buildings seemed to roll by for my education. Peaceful in the motion of the river, I floated like baby Moses starting a pilgrimage through God's green plantation.

I began at that time to have visions of the human body as it corresponds, part for part, to the entire cosmos. Our bodies and the mystery of Christ interpenetrating one another with the constant modulations of the four elements. I realize now that all the visions I collected in *Liber divinorum operum* began with the glorious epiphany on the water.[5]

But in the daily world such moments are short-lived. I became aware of the barrenness, thirst, and confusion in so many sisters and brothers unsure of their vocations; chaos in houses where leadership had failed; and frequent neglect of the exquisite, detailed beauties on which the momentum of liturgy depends. Instead of going on pilgrimage for refreshment, I became part of the waterway somehow connecting people to Christ's faraway limbs, instilling in them a hunger for the real source and a discernment forswearing the substitutes that are offered.

Oh, I saw Cistercian industry, evidence of hard physical work, ancient Benedictine raised beds beautifully tended, some breathtaking frescoes and sculpted images of Our Lady, monumental uses of stone and glass that rival the splendor of visionary beauty, but the insides of many of the churches were desiccated, and the nobility of exemplary clergy was nowhere found.

An ability I had noted in myself, being able to carry on in two modes simultaneously, was exercised to the limit when I was traveling. My outer senses were bombarded every day anew with architectures, dialects, machines, costumes, and operations I had never met before. Those I received soaked into me naturally, but there was no time for reflecting on them. Meanwhile I was inspired by God in many utterances from that part of my soul most connected to the divine mysteries. The first time I had not even brought a scribe with me, and I lacked time and energy for recording thoughts.

As my senses registered colors, shapes, and sounds, I was called upon to arbitrate monastic disputes. I advised a prioress about the choice of Lenten readings for her women, corrected faulty psalmody for singers struggling without a trained cantor, but did more speaking than singing. I grew hoarse, and craved silence.

A cascade of deaths has been so much our witness these last years, death comes more and more as a familiar. First Volmar left us, barely four years ago, which forced me to complete a most complex book of visions without his perennial encouragement and exactitude. Next came the death of the young monk Godfrey; most recently, my own brother Hugo. Each one of them was a true servant of God who dutifully came to be our provost, my secretary and scribe.

I am long too old and wise to linger over the thought that the death of any one human being radically alters the shape of the cosmos; yet, as microcosm of that larger sphere, the spirit that is Volmar has not been replaced. I feel his presence and register his loss as one and the same, living and blessed. The first time Volmar spoke to me about his wish to be buried in our orchard—shyly, I thought, after all our years of intimate work—I gave little thought to his conscious breach of customary practice. More than twenty years had passed since his duties as provost had made St. Rupertsberg his home rather than St. Disibode, where he had made his profession as Benedictine monk. His residence with us had been hard-won, wearing even further the already threadbare relationship between ourselves and our former abbot Kuno at Disibodenberg, but Volmar's unquestioning loyalty to us was impeccable and his service still in a sense irreplaceable. From the early days before we moved here, he received the urgencies of my mind as fully as any mortal has been able. He never failed to support its fullest expression, to transcribe with highest human accuracy my Latin grammar, syntax, and rhetoric while holding fast to the divine authorship that spoke through me.

In all best ways I was able to learn from him as he served me, and my own command of the language has grown so strong that I will never again be in the risky position of scribal dependence I once felt. Now, one who is asked to serve as secretary-scribe receives a more polished product from the very first. I wrote as much to Guibert[6] before he came here, eager to see whether this condition cooled his zeal to serve us as scribe and provost. I have not been disappointed, nor, he claims, is he.

More indirectly, I learned from Volmar in ways he could not know. His educated visitors became mine as well. He became a trusted conduit to knowledge in the larger monastic world of men. Information flowed and I was a recipient—remarkable for one of my gender, even as abbess. It never would have occurred to him to be resentful of my growing authority; rather, he counted himself the beneficiary, the more equality we achieved. Without this I would never have been so well prepared for the world I encountered on various preaching tours. The politics of the clergy did not take me by surprise. The worldliness of the hierarchy I knew partially through Basel of Cologne, through my blood brother Hugo, and through a year of bitter skirmishes with Rikkarda's brother, the high-handed archbishop. Most of all I knew it from visitors and my opportunities to discuss the news they carried, whether it was of emperor, pope, antipope, or of the schools in Paris—all in confidence of Volmar's absolute trust. Rare, privileged friendship!

We knew Godfrey so briefly; he did not grow with us. When his services had been requested, St. Disibode's Abbot Helengerus was again unwilling to provide what our old agreement had so clearly stated (Volmar's burial with us no doubt the latest grievance against us). Not until I had appealed to Pope Alexander himself, who prevailed upon my own nephew Wezelin to arbitrate the dispute,[7] did the inconstant abbot agree to send us Godfrey,[8] adding to the young monk's duties a mandate to begin setting down the spiritual *vita* of the old abbess! I remember chuckling to myself when I learned this. Clearly Helengerus must think (or hope) me ready for the buzzards. It must surely seem strange that I am alive and stirring troubled waters after so many bouts of illness. Who could have imagined these tired joints might outperform so many spry and heartier bodies?

But no sooner had we achieved a measure of understanding between us and made visible progress on the *vita*—establishing an alternation between his narrative reports and contributions from me explaining the nature of my visions, their time of onset in early life, and the reason for my painful delays in revealing them—than young Godfrey himself took fever and predeceased me. We could not save him, but relinquished his body with care to his community for burial.

My brother Hugo came unexpectedly at news of Godfrey's death, presided at a Requiem Mass honoring both Volmar and Godfrey, then surprised me further by arranging permission from Mainz to fill temporarily the deep well Volmar had carved as provost and secretary. The joy of having Hugo join in our own music was unlooked-for, and the best medicine to move me through my first weeks without Godfrey.

Hugo was already in a monastic school by the time our parents gave me to Jutta for raising when I was eight. Memories of our playing or being friends at home before I left are not even retrievable, it is so long ago. I do recall a story—perhaps from letters—about Hugo's love of singing, a report that brought joy to all the family at home. There were virtually no letters between Hugo and me as we each pursued our religious vocations. Only as abbess of our separate community did I have opportunity to learn more of the inner circle of Mainz Cathedral and celebrate the news that he had been appointed to the office of cantor. Basel knew him thus, and made it a practice to keep me apprised of news of Hugo when anything came to his ears.

Not only Godfrey's, but Hugo's service with us here at Rupertsberg was as brief as Volmar's was lasting. Unexpectedly, my brother Hugo was taken with the same fever as Godfrey, violent and uncompromising; he died in our own dispensary, held in my hands. That, in its own way, was a rare privilege.

This time I chose to circumvent the time-honored truculence of Abbot Helengerus altogether, and we now find ourselves with a curious Walloon monk who had determinedly petitioned to serve as secretary-scribe before he was even invited. We work well together, and daily Guibert gains my confidence in his thirst to understand and grasp full-blown the spillings of a soul Volmar knew from its struggling infancy.

Guibert has maintained, from his first days here as scribe, that a community of our standing, with two monastic houses to its credit and an abbess whose advice is still sought by correspondents from all ranks, should include a *glossa ordinaria* among its holdings. He managed the loan of a glossed Bible for us to copy in the scriptorium, and it has provided a focus of my teaching for several years. As important glosses are completed, I have them read at refectory. The commentary is schooling for all of us, but when my women ask questions about it, I am amazed. Mostly I have no idea what they take in and can learn of reasoned commentary. We are not schoolmen, after all, whose livelihoods depend on training their minds to reasoned argument and rhetoric.

These commentaries are produced by such finely disciplined minds and are a part of the history and tradition we share as monastics in the body of Christ. Glosses draw not only from the beloved Church fathers whose thinking we know from our Matins readings—bits of sermons and exegesis, for example—but also from trusted monastic luminaries like Venerable Bede, and like Walafrid Strabo and his great teacher Rabanus Maurus, who are responsible for the glosses on the Acts of the Apostles. Not until our own times were all these varied writings compiled, fitted together like the pieces of an immense puzzle by the learned Anselm of the cathedral school at Laon.

I am not certain that I subscribe to Guibert's estimation of the value of a glossed Bible as a permanent record for our community, since contributions are still added and changes still made, from what I hear. That is always a problem with writing things down on valued parchment. In the end, only the Vulgate and the canonical texts of Mass and Office are definitive; nevertheless, I have been willing to follow his advice so far as the copying is concerned. It is true that, as my women complete portions in the scriptorium and bring them to me for inspection, the pages are a form of beauty unto themselves.

Without paintings or color, the shapes glosses form on the page are striking. The design of each page is unique, although the text of the Vulgate itself always occupies the same place in the center. Commentaries form borders—wide above and below the central text, narrower on the two sides, and it is always a challenge to puzzle out the exact spatial requirement of the gloss. In addition, the Vulgate we have glossed—one we acquired from an earlier time—was written in another script, not the one we teach our women for scribal duties. This adds another degree of variety to the design, and since I have been unwilling to wait for one consistent hand to struggle through the entire course of Old and New Testaments, patriarchs and prophets, we now have the further variety of having had several individual hands to the task.

Their dedication has frankly surprised me, and it has provided a rich book for the community. Christina of course inquired early in the project why I had not myself written any commentary on the Vulgate, and whether I might yet do so. She couched the latter in terms of leaving space in case there were additions I would want to make. I wasn't certain whether she might be starting one of her disruptive spells, and I instructed her to proceed with assigning and administering the copying of the commentaries exactly as they presented themselves in the copy

Guibert had borrowed for our use. I considered the subject finished when I dismissed her.

However, as has so often occurred between Christina and myself, her questioning had already worked its way into my thinking, and it hatched many more questions in turn. It is only in the past few years, in my extreme old age, that I have begun to consider at all the nature of what I have written in my lifetime and what I *haven't* written.

Serious consideration began, I know, with Godfrey's investigations for my *vita* (unfinished, and abandoned at his death). Then came Guibert's gently probing questions about the nature of my visions—their genesis and frequency, the source for their authority, and their effect on my person. Until the two men began questioning me about these things, I had not thought to describe them, but only to give form to the powerful experiences themselves, to give voice to the Voice of Wisdom as it speaks through me. Such consciousness of self and the nature of the work produced can be extremely dangerous, and it was with great reluctance that I finally assigned it importance.

Now that I do consider these things in the same wonder and humility with which I directly experience them, Christina's question is valid. After all, I have indeed written other commentary, and I can't honestly say that it comes from the same fiery place as the music, the visions, the prophecy. For instance, the commentaries on the Rule of St. Benedict and on the Athanasian Creed:[9] they are not from beyond me, nor has experience of them transported me. Basel would probably have called them reasoned pedagogy, like the works of clerics who are also schoolmen, of monks and even priests who are also theologians. So why not commentary on the Vulgate?

August 15, 1178
Feast of the Assumption of the Virgin

I love seeing them bent over the table, copying the rounded script, rubricating the initials so we can more easily locate beginnings and endings on the page. Even the smells are heady, like incense. The powder that dissolves into ink is strangely acrid, even in its dry state. When the liquid is added, its pungent odor is unmistakable for anything else: it is learning, industry, beauty, and commitment.

The greatest difficulty is the light. Soon after we began the scriptorium, I discovered that morning work period was a good time, and I would set them to work immediately following Terce. Light poured in through the three small east-facing windows. From Advent until about the middle of Lent the first year was a perfect beginning. They began to complain before Easter, and by Pentecost I feared either open rebellion or blindness. The sun, now so much more directly overhead, never found an angled entrance into our workroom at all, and I hadn't really planned against that. None of the other activities we regularly practiced were so demanding of our eyes. Even weaving becomes a remarkably regular, nearly kinesthetic practice, once the warp and woof are threaded and decisions are made about organizing the pattern. Following that, its perfection then depends on strength and fluidity of motion—the development of a rhythmic sense of what the pattern demands—rather than the perfect coordination of eye and hand. But the exactitude of copying requires not only fluency in the skills of forming and joining individual letters, but also the sympathetic understanding among eyes, intelligence, and hand that will admit to constant surprises, unexpected turnings—an ability to proceed without the regularity that fixed patterning provides. Only a few of my women had a natural aptitude for this work, and discovering who else could be trained to master it has been a maddening process of trial and error for all of us. I could ill afford failure to provide satisfactory working conditions for those few who showed promise.

We tried remedies, none of which solved the problem to anyone's satisfaction. Candles dripped onto the costly sheets and gave off such a flickering light that accuracy was badly compromised. They brought me several sheets of good vellum whose rubbings-out and errant script rendered them unacceptable for anything other than practice, a luxury ill-afforded, especially that first year. By then the weather was warm, however, and I instructed them to try out of doors. That meant the sturdy table had to be transported each time, which aroused the predictable complaints, but they made the effort. As I recall, I had them recite Latin case endings in loud voice as they lifted and carried, to give joint momentum as well as to preclude the possibility of individual vain utterances. It cheered them on, and they became more cooperative. One or two were enthusiastic. Birgit even devised a clever carrying tray, constructed of heavy, quite stiff cowhide. She designed it with compartments to hold inkpot, rule, quills, and gums.

We were encouraged, but briefly. No sooner would they organize themselves outside than capricious breezes instantly materialized. Valuable ink was spilled onto precious vellum. A newly finished sheet wafted into the freshly manured kitchen garden before the page was sufficiently dry to weight and stack. The weather was entirely too unpredictable, and the quality of work deteriorated. The activity became more like a game, and one day I found them handing around a drying sheet like a relay team batting with the wind that caught and filled it like a sail. It was proving better for physical exercise than for the development of their minds and eyes, and I somewhat reluctantly moved them back inside.

It was then I found a liturgical blessing for our scriptorium and knew it was needed to refocus their scattered energies and sacralize the work itself. It was simple enough, and they had committed it to memory after a single recitation. Next, I had Christina provide us with a piece of linen too worn for its original purpose. Using brushes rather than quills, I had three of them render copies, promising that the finest would be draped like a banner to adorn the scriptorium:

> Grace with blessing, Lord,
> this thy family's place of writings,
> so its members comprehend what they write
> and perfect it in their works.[10]

We were all inspired anew. The best of the copies was mounted on the wall, and we began to experiment with solutions to the problem of light. We found, first of all, that it was worth using our best beeswax candles rather than the cheap tallow. They burned more evenly, and they dripped less, which is why we had heretofore reserved them for liturgical use, to protect Volmar's missal. Further improvement came with the use of oil lamps: either fish or plant oil gave off the steadiest light we had so far found, and the saucer placed on the table gave a suitable radiance to a large enough area. The women became thoroughly engaged in trying different oils and kept a tally of the comparative advantages of each. Instead of reporting to me each day, I had them note the results on wax tablets. They were improving their orthography and punctuation as they studied the physical problem.

Sometime during all this I was called on another preaching tour. At Trier, in the community of my dear friend Abbot Ludwig,[11] I saw the finest scriptorium I had so far witnessed and there observed a different procedure, kinder to the eyes and less exacting of light. Instead of laboriously copying the strokes, abbreviations, letters, and punctuations of a borrowed text, Abbot Ludwig's monks sat at quiet attention as one brother, gifted with a richly cadenced voice, recited the text. His delivery was slow and careful, his rhetorical skills at dictation nearly forming the letters with his lips, the scribes transcribing the sounds with the physical ease of trained cats, at once so relaxed, attentive, and gathered in the energy they applied to the task. The contrast between this activity—its contemplative quality—and that of our scriptorium thus far was instructive, and I tucked this important piece of learning into a recess of my own memory for safekeeping.

But as I recall, I exhausted myself on that particular tour and returned to do battle with one of the worst bouts of illness I had suffered in some years. I was able to give little attention to practical details. It was weeks after returning before I was well enough to resume activities in the scriptorium, because nothing outside the blessed ritual seems to go forward in my absence. Between the tour itself, plus the time for recuperation, it was nearly Advent when we resumed, and the light was with us once again.

I began at that point to allow the practices of morning chapter and afternoon work period to interact most exactly with one another. In the morning we would read a chapter of the Rule as we regularly did, with my full commentary on its particulars and principles. After Terce, in the scriptorium, the same chapter would be read by one sister and then taken down by several others, who were then *learning* the Rule as they learned to *read and write* the Rule. We could be true to our inscription. Their reading as well as their writing skills improved so significantly that by the time of Lent, when it is customary according to our Rule for me to assign each of them a text for private reading, those who had performed scribal duties for their work period were not overwhelmed by the task I set them. This fact was not lost on the others, and, for the first time, I had more than half a dozen requests for scribal duties. We had turned a corner.

When I observe them now, so many years later, practiced and able, I need to remind myself how gradual was the accretion of skills. I honestly do not remember at what point the activity acquired its seasonal nature. As Charlemagne's chief schoolmaster, the monk Alcuin had centuries before reinforced the dignified status of scribal labor. He insisted that it be accorded legitimacy as full equivalent of the manual labor prescribed for us all under St. Benedict's Rule. Here was that rare species, a manual work with full equivalency under the Rule that women could perform as well as men. According to the Rule, the length of time as well as the particular tasks for manual labor change from winter to summer. Even more important is the prescribed seasonal change in the hour for the night office and its proximity to Lauds and Prime. So also with our scribal procedures.

From Advent through Lent the bulk of our copying is done, when the light is best and the women are grateful to work inside. We are able to produce multiple copies by dictating: when they are assigned to the scriptorium they must already be skilled in the comprehension that turns what comes through the ear into intelligible inked shapes.

Production of multiple copies is an important means of increasing our library, since we are thereby in a better position to barter with other monastic libraries. By the time a work is slowly and carefully read aloud, it is also written, in triplicate if not quadruplicate. Financing sufficient vellum is our only difficulty. From Easter through the long days of Pentecost, we do most of the binding, with the occasional illuminating of single sheets and rubrication of particular initials that can be accomplished wherever the light happens to be best, supplemented by the aid of oil lamps as necessary.

Of course each woman responds differently, just as they are gifted so differently, but there are always a few who—as they catch on to the skills—reveal in their eyes and increasingly fluid surety of hand-movement the deep mystery that enlivens the very transmission of these ancient, sacred texts.

September 8, 1178
Feast of the Nativity of the Virgin

After Compline, I thought to check the fair copy of the epistle prepared by Christina for the messenger who comes regularly now at first light. It was stunning to see the aberrant additions she had made. Schematic geometric diagrams and florid designs wound around and even through the text of the page. Single words were decorated. Her own name was somehow elaborated through two of the designs, and four crude German words were pointedly positioned at thc corners of the page.

Briefly I wondered where and at what age she could have heard such worldly eruptions of language, what her experience of them might have been. Only in detaching myself from such useless speculations did I begin to sense the agitation of body that signaled the tortuous pullings and feverish disruptions of the mind and hand that produced these strange illuminations. I turned the parchment upside down, and further disordered designs fell into place, aggressively moving into the text at unpredictable spots through cutting strokes of the pen. Now it was unmistakable: male organs wagged at me.

And now my ever failing memory for detail recollects a similar instance eight years ago, at the end of my fourth preaching tour. I had traveled to twenty-one different monastic and cathedral communities that time and returned fully spent, already trying to ignore early stages of one of the most severe attacks of illness I had sustained. I battled the growing pressures behind the eyes, the ringing in one ear, vertigo and nausea and occasional, violent attacks of vomiting, but hoped that the regularity of our daily round would restore me. The disrupted schedule I pursued while on tour was enough to unbalance anyone's system! The food at several places was unfamiliar and often far too rich, the timing of Offices sometimes unpredictable or unpredictably shortened. My soul was cheated while my stomach floundered, and it is always difficult for me to sleep away from my private quarters, where flowers in season and gatherings of dried lavender, thyme, and hay-scented fern bouquet the space with an odor that is soporific in the dark. Sleepless nights away found me fussing over laxities in the liturgy, infractions in musical practice, or disheveled psalmody at Office that obliterated the powerful texts and offended sensitized ears.

Although my prioress was in charge while I was traveling, it had long been our practise for Christina to organize and supervise the work done in the scriptorium, whether it was instruction in letters or the actual copying of texts. Her energy for the task was remarkable, and, in addition to her long-developed talent with ink pen and paintbrush, she was skillful at apportioning tasks, spotting minor talents, and minimizing with natural enthusiasm and good humor the petty, competitive tendencies among the women regularly at work there. While it might have been my preference to have all illumination and rubrication painted by Christina alone, she wisely developed a more generous sharing of the beauty-filled tasks in the scriptorium, thereby encouraging the talents of others.

We all suffered periods when Christina's normally energetic manner approached belligerence. She might interrupt the speech of her sisters during recreation, and women who had happily worked under her tutelage in the scriptorium would come to me in bewilderment, reporting a terrible and abrupt fragmentation in the tasks she assigned to them. She not only rushed all of them, they reported, but she switched them from one manuscript to another, resulting in impossible junctures of text, for which she would then fault them.

Usually these periods lasted not more than a week or two, and they abated with additional prayer and rest. As soon as I was aware that her balance was tipping, I would find reasons to reduce the demands for fair copy from the scriptorium. No letters would be sent out for a short time; Christina's responsibilities would then be reduced to supervising the workroom while some of the women made an inventory of supplies, determined what needed replenishing in the way of vellum, colors, and glues, and decided what of that we could produce ourselves from plants and mordants and what we required from outside. Soon Christina's characteristic attention to detail and careful guidance would mercifully return, and activity in the scriptorium would resume its cheerful, productive, bustling pace.

But her behavior that time when I lay so ill and exhausted from travel was entirely different from such periodic wafts of exaggeration. I could not bear to hear of squabbles and jealousies, or of the despair that follows those that fall into old habits of fear, and had instructed my prioress that I was not to be disturbed for anything. I prayed that the grace of God would restore my health as it had so many times before, observed the regularity of our bells with a joy that overrode pains, and sang the Office alone in my quarters. Only for daily Mass would I allow them to carry me into the church, and I even directed Volmar to preside at chapter of faults in my place.

By the time I was strong enough to navigate on my own legs and attend to the accumulation of responsibilities that awaited me, reports of Christina's actions were alarming. Not only was her supervisory behavior in the scriptorium frenetic and difficult to follow for those she directed; this time, sister portress twice had discovered Christina wandering the gardens in the fading light after Compline. She reported seeing Christina leaping in silhouette between the raised beds. There was no reasoning with Christina. She had no business on the grounds during the Great Silence, but my portress describes finally having to wrestle with Christina after nearly an hour of more gentle physical urging. At the second occurrence, Christina had become more destructive of living things around her. She had yanked great bunches of leeks, beets, and turnips from the raised beds. Then, as the portress approached, turned furtively and—in the way a dog or wolf might do—dug furiously with paddled hands and forearms in order to rebury at designated locations the vegetables she had pulled on her rampage. It took several hours and had long since turned dark by the time our portress was able to get Christina back into the house and to her own cell. From there she was able to get help from our infirmarian, who, with permission from sister prioress, administered medicinals to ensure that Christina would sleep, and deeply.

As she reported all of this to me, I noted how portress, prioress, and infirmarian all concurred in their amazement at the physical strength displayed by Christina in this state. Obedience can hold no sway over such unreasoning and disordered energy; I pray and think deeply now about the precautions I need to take in order to keep Christina in our fold. I shall begin by destroying the letter I hold in my hand.

October 18, 1178
Feast of St. Luke, Evangelist

Last night the oldest man I have ever seen appeared in my dream. His face resembled one of those withered apples we sometimes unearth in the storeroom at the end of winter. I placed hands on his face, fingered the surfaces of planes and valleys, sharp mountain ridges and river beds, as if some vast knowledge of history and geography could be gleaned through the hands. At first I could understand nothing of what he was saying. It was as if he spoke in a tongue I had never heard before. I could sense a beautiful rhetoric to his speech—parallel clauses, clear cadences, perfectly clear points of structure; still, I didn't understand a word. As I was attending these rather musical qualities, everything shifted, and I understood his language; either that, or he suddenly was speaking mine. However it happened, I could hear he was speaking of the uses of age. Once again I understood nothing for a time, then the language was clear, almost the way things can come in and out of focus to the eye.

Hours later the sensations remain in my hands. If I were a sculptor and could work wood or clay, the sensations in my hands could become knowledge again and recreate such a face and head. So God molded Adam out of earth and breathed life into him. But I can no longer attempt to mold young life. God created Adam out of His own perfection, young, vigorous, with ears sensible to every possible sound, including the movements of the spheres and the layering of minerals. All this Adam could reproduce—not with his hands, but as pure sound from his throat, every subtlety of every sound in its rhythmic flow. Such perfection is nearly unimaginable to me, so abstract, with no physical sensibilities, an infinite panoply of sound. Even my visions have had more limitations, forms, colors, and edges.

I have barely touched such perfection in my lifetime—conducting chant, teaching the *Ordo virtutum*[12] as one long musical line, or insisting on all the connections at the Paschal Vigil among the Exultet, the Exodus, and the institution of Bread and Wine. Even doing that, I am aware of the enormous human limitations—the bodies in all shapes and sizes, rebellious thoughts, petty jealousies, and self-involvements.

As for Adam's youthful vigor, the cornucopia of energy that knows no bounds and imagines everything to be possible, like our youngest postulants who have sought us out eager to measure themselves against the Rule, these no longer excite me. Except as instances of sheer beauty, youth no longer interests me. I seek the knowledge encoded in the face of the ancient of my dream, somehow sensible to my hands that have anointed the sick and dying and blessed monstrous infants and women tortured in birthing. And the knowledge in Rikkarda's hands turning me on my sickbed, Basel's hands with their spatulate fingers, and Volmar's faithful hands recording until death the words that came through me.

Part Two

October 21, 1178
Feast of St. Ursula and the 11,000 Virgins

Christina recovered is northeast storm transformed into western wind. It is as though any of the evil eruptions were unthinkable. She is cheerful, eager to work, and filled with sisterly love. In all my years as abbess, no one else has exhibited such a capacity for things of visual beauty—whether creating likenesses, calligraphs, geometric patterns, or fanciful plants or animals.

She has passed her twenty-fifth year of religious life with us, yet approaches her later years without having visibly aged. In her person there is always a quality of fresh green shoots that sprout from a bulb in early March. She brims with plans and dreams for the decoration of manuscripts. I have only to encourage her by a word of permission granted or directive given, and she responds like a spring-freshened brook. Images of leaves, beasts, flowers bubble up and out of her pen and brush, seeming to take on life in a way that is sometimes disquieting in its closeness to taking the sacred breath of life for its own.

We have spoken privately at regular intervals over our years together, and it is clear that her intelligence is generous and deep. But Wisdom does not seek her out. I have often attempted to explain to her the distinction between symbols and graven images, the fine line of discernment between being spoken through and skillfully capturing one's own particular desires as beauty. I sense so strongly that the evil forces periodically seizing her, wreaking such havoc in our house, gain entrance through her lack of discernment.

When she is in balance, she steadfastly will not recall the times of seizure. It is as if such things never happened to her: she cannot imagine who might have destroyed one-third of last year's kitchen garden or obdurately refused my instructions to return to her cell late at night during Great Silence, screaming foul abuse through the cloister. When she is restored to health, she is organized, kind, and almost too demonstrative on the surface. Many times I have needed to call to mind my own painful experience with Rikkarda, the detachment I have developed over the years that allows me to be evenhanded with the difficulties my women eternally present. Nor does she push hard to invade my necessary detachment, for deep within Christina there is a fear that scurries to remain hidden.

That terrible fear gnaws at her, chews away at her, eventually makes her wakeful and exhausts her. It is like a perversion of the story of the wise and foolish virgins, for it is not that she loses faith and falls asleep; rather, she is perpetually wakeful and visited not by Caritas but by a demon lover who then torments us all through her. Over the years I have come to recognize signs of approaching eruptions—her eyes glitter unnaturally, her voice gets louder, with too much laughter too often, her temper shortens, and finally she has no patience left at all. Yet having seen the signs, I have never been able to ward off the eruption nor predict either its course or longevity.

Exorcism is not in order. It is not possession, and it leaves much more abruptly than it comes on; in fact, it leaves without a trace, as you and I discussed so many times, Volmar. Now, for instance, my old friend, you should see her—at her best and as we both most admired her. She has inquired again about illuminating my old catalog of the natural world. How she would excel at painting miniatures of all our birds, each metal in its characteristic permutations of color, and of course the trees. This time I am more inclined than ever to concur and long to speak with you at length about it. I value your opinion.

As we take up a good investigation of the beneficial plants next Lenten season, imagine how the potency of each green plant would be underscored by eternalizing its beauty on parchment, emphasizing its peculiar shape, noting the texture of smooth or hairy leaves, rounded or toothed at their edges, gray-green more of air or brown-green of the earth. And do the leaves of a particular plant arrange themselves in opposite or alternate pairs, or does any one leaf really comprise dozens of smaller joined pieces? What of its efflorescence? Any who come after us who are not skilled at reading Latin script could depend on our taxonomy by its skilled renderings in lines and colors.

I wonder sometimes whether I am alone in needing to see *all* of the created universe interrelated. Our great theologians have assiduously studied and clarified the four-fold meanings of the Vulgate—the literal, allegorical, moral, and anagogical. They have skillfully traced the epiphanic roots in the Old Testament that prefigure the divine manifestation of the New. Wisdom has brought me further elucidations of divine mysteries in our own time and interpreted symbols of daunting complexity. Yet, since I see all in all, I must bring forth the connections between parts of the human body and those of the universe, as I did in *De operatione dei.*[13] I must see the shape of the cosmos as it is progressively revealed to me, for it has changed from its stratified egg shape to that of an orb pierced by the Godhead.

Our Bible is glossed, the great central text chewed, digested, and elucidated by the best-educated minds from our Church, gleaned from centuries of enlightened reasoning. Little of that comes from the monastic life, however, and it is the hallmark of our Benedictine way that liturgy and vocation tie us to the earth from which Adam was carved and to which we all return as dust. The divine mysteries of the natural world reveal themselves in the contemplative life. The strength of the sun as it limns the veins of a leaf, the moon's watery appearance on a dark night as a path of phosphorescence in the river, these elicit our voices of praise. Throughout my long life and especially in my latest years I have yearned to see this divine love of the Creator for the created rendered in the beauty of paint and poetry. At the end I question whether such ever changing subtleties can be frozen on flat sheets, but rather are only lived liturgically. That possibility will never be acceptable to Christina, nor can I adequately explain it; yet surely by now she has felt the limits of her hands.

November 23, 1178
Feast of St. Clement, Pope and Martyr

We buried a young nobleman on the Feast of St. Luke, putting him to rest in the southwest corner of our cemetery. As I recall, it was one of those last extraordinary days of autumn when butter-yellow linden, red of maple, and bronze of oak converge in a triumphant blaze of glory, so that our eyes were dazzled as we sang a hymn by the side of his grave. Since he was not one of us, we had not had his body with us for a vigil or the full Requiem Mass in our own church, but we honored him with an Office for the Dead. Guibert presided at the grave, and I gave a blessing. A simple wooden marker, flush with the earth, recorded his name and dates.

Everything about that sunfilled day seemed orderly and appropriate until, just a few days after the burial, I heard from Mainz—in fact from clerics acting on behalf of their absent archbishop, Christian—that our young man was excommunicate: he had been severed from the Church some time ago, did not merit Christian burial, and must immediately be exhumed from his place with us.

I have no doubt that obedience is required of me by virtue of my office. The only question is, obedience to whom? After making inquiries, I was told the young man had been not only excommunicated but also formally reconciled by a priest several months before his untimely death. More to the point, any remaining doubts that might have clouded my judgment were removed for me in a powerful vision demanding my obedience to God, a higher order than obedience to Mainz. The divine words in the vision were clear: we had buried his body in our sacred ground, honored him with our prayers and psalms in full accord with the customs of our Rule, and there he deserves his rest; to exhume the body, to tear it from its resting place with us, would be an act of sacrilege.

Assured in the vision that obedience required our protection of the young man, I wrote accordingly, and the letter was sent off promptly to Mainz.

Initially I had not informed my women about the exchange of letters, since any ripple of scandal to one of our houses elicits exaggerated attention. It seemed possible that the demand from Mainz was based on lack of information about his reconciliation, in which case my quick response would settle their anxieties. But it was not to be. Only this morning another letter from Mainz repeats the demand. Threatens us with an interdict that would deprive us of singing the Divine Office and of receiving the Eucharist. The records show he was excommunicate at time of death, they argue.

Their sources are spurious, yet they stand firm. I fear this is a clerical show of force. I am much too old to be troubled by the machinations of worldly prelates, but my obedience must be to God and the sacraments of Jesus Christ. I will neither exhume the body nor allow anyone else to tear the corpse from our cemetery. The marker will simply not be found.

It is time to share the awful knowledge with the full community and pray for strength without song. Dear Mother of God, if Volmar's presence is with us still, bring it closer, so that I may lean on him a little. I do not need guidance, only support and the strength of our years combined.

December 3, 1178
First Sunday in Advent

This morning Wilhelmina wants to know whether she obeys the interdict, because she hears each of the melodies of the Divine Office even though we no longer sing them.

I had not thought it could be otherwise, since I too hear all that we are forbidden to sing. I taste the body and blood we are forbidden to swallow. It had not occurred to me that there might be some of my women who would not hear the divine praise, for whom silencing the outer sounds would silence the inner ones as well. It is not something I ever thought to discuss with them. The sounds made by the movement of the heavenly spheres exist whether or not we have the ears to hear them. Choirs of angels make their joyful noise regardless of who is privileged to listen.

Being deeply embodied, we feel our humanity rendered senseless under such an interdict. But not faithless, nor are we without spiritual resources. We will obey our archbishop, suffering in silence: but the sound of praise goes on all over the Christian world, and at the appointed hours we are not forbidden to listen.

I was not able to reassure Wilhelmina; she experiences the inner song as a temptation. She asked about a possible penance. She is a gifted singer, strong and sensitive. When it is her turn to cantor, she leads us well; now she thrashes in a sea of guilt.

I am sure the penance she seeks is a stringent fast. Her zeal for mortifying the flesh is well known to us. She thinks she would still the inner voice by deadening the bodily responses to nourishment. Robbed of its natural outlet of physical sound, her desire is naked and frightens her. Already suffering painfully the loss of exercising a considerable natural gift, she is newly conscious of the energetic desire after beauty that drives it. Now she renames it temptation and hopes to still it with willful self-rule. Better yet if I impose a stringent penance: that way willfulness becomes obedience.

Fortunately the body, inspirited by God, has the wisdom to feed itself on nourishment it has already stored, and just so the soul receives nourishment from both inner and outer experiences of divine beauty called to mind in meditation or silent prayer. Thus are we able to survive for surprising lengths of time on what our souls have stored in memory.

We deceive ourselves in imagining that matter can be understood as inherently evil, and would find ourselves rapidly approaching heresy, like gnostic Cathars. I have always known that; living closely with trees, observing the seasons, collecting medicinals, and seeing the blossom in its seed are good. God in His wisdom could not have created evil, nor would He have embodied His word in matter if it were an unworthy host. This has always been perfectly clear to me.

But I do remember floundering in confusion about inner knowledge, for years tormented by the possibility that my visions might be a temptation to sin. At first it was innocent enough. As a youngster I was visited periodically by bathings of celestial light and gold-washed images that shifted with dizzying speed. As I matured, I learned these experiences isolated me even from Jutta and, later, from Volmar, my trusted guides. I wondered whether I was welcoming the company of God or of the devil.

I was always careful not to be seeking after the experiences, but they found me open. Rounds and rounds of psalms cradled in changing antiphons and continual singing of choral Propers to the Mass produced vibrational buzzing in the bones of my cheeks, nose, and jaw, *et lingua mea adhaesit faucibus meis,* with tongue cleaved to the roof of my mouth.

Then there might be the flickering movement of yellow flames as we processed—all with poised attention. I saw fluid-focused details and wholes, fine points and firmament. It was like being the fruit ripening on the tree, exuding more and more fragrance, color deepening, until quite suddenly I became aware of fruit flesh expanding and its hard kernels so many precise forms of knowledge bombarding from within. What name should I give the tree, how to call it? Tree of knowledge of good and evil? Judas-tree, rood, or devil's delight? Why gather me, bathe me in such intense light only to throw me down the rock-lined precipice? I had lived more than half this long life before I stopped fearing the company of Lucifer. Somewhere in the middle I began to understand that temptation to sin was not the goad at all but, rather, temptation to doubt God's guidance—to imagine that I could be the one to determine who is worthy to receive or what gifts of knowledge are possible. Already in the second century, Irenaeus knew that "error come by a tree was righted by the tree of obedience when, hearing his God, the Son of man stood nailed upon a tree: knowledge of evil thrown aside, knowledge of good did enter wide, and rooted."[14]

Thank God I do not so torture myself any longer. Wisdom has built herself a house in me, has set up her tent here, and my very old age has afforded the rare privilege of growing more and more intimate with her. Having outlived my dearest friends and few human guides, I bask in the light of my present company with remarkable surety. Wisdom's Voice drew me down to the cemetery, inhabited my abbatial staff that led me to the very spot where we had interred the body of the reconciled sinner; in fact, two pairs of her long wings cradled me while the third pair swept the ground clean of any mark that could identify the location of that young man's presence in our orchard. No marks, no doubt; it was remarkably simple; Thy rod and Thy staff.

December 28, 1178
Feast of the Holy Innocents

The joy of Christ's birth escapes us all in the dark, dying days of December, closing this year of enforced silence. My women ail, and I am brought low by my old illness and excessive age. We are exiles, they and I, in our own house; exiled from our life's work of sung praise.

According to the liturgical calendar that gives us life, we are this week in the company of Christ's nobility: St. Stephen, the first of His obedient martyrs; St. John, His beloved disciple, obedient unto death; this day all those Holy Innocents too young even to know they were slaughtered without reason by a madman; and crowned tomorrow by the feast of our newest martyr, England's lamentably murdered Archbishop Thomas.

How public the events surrounding the exile and martyrdom of Archbishop Thomas, and how clear they now appear. Our own struggle smolders, and the entire community suffers shame and exile at the hands of our clerical superiors. I reverence the soul of the man who took up Canterbury's staff, thereby renouncing deep friendship and royal favor in order to lead his flock according to the true light. Never in my lifetime have the events of a human's martyrdom swept through all of Christendom with such speed: murdered at the altar of his own cathedral on the morrow of December in the year of our Lord 1170 with four of his first biographers witness to the event; canonized by the true pope late in February a mere two years later, with his king's public penance the year following—Henry II humbling himself as only one barefoot man among the throng of pilgrims that daily flock to Thomas's shrine.[15]

I knew some time ago of the shock created by Thomas's unexpected struggle with his king, from the time that Henry named him, but now I find myself looking at martyrdom anew, from the vantage point of exile. I will never forget. It was on my last preaching tour, in the south, in Swabia, nearly ten years ago. I was already too old for dragging my bones to unknown places. It was cold and damp, much too early in the fall for that kind of weather, but there it was. I was not the only stranger; an honored monk from Gaul was also present, and when a fire had been lit in the common room, he closed his eyes and began to sing of Thomas Becket's exile:

> In Rama a cry goes up
>   from the weeping Rachel of England,
> For a son of Herod
>   shames her:
> Behold how her first-born,
>   the Joseph of Canterbury,
> is in exile as if sold,
>   and he lives in the Egypt of France.[16]

Today's Communion text brought it all back to me, the grief for the innocents:

> A voice was heard in Rama, lamentation and great mourning;
> it was Rachel weeping for her children, and she would not be comforted, because none is left.[17]

For us, my surprisingly loyal women and I, it is very much like living in exile, since we are deprived of the most sacred elements—His body and blood in the Communion and music of praise in both Mass and Office. We are agonized in this banishment: I live only for our return, and my determination is unquestioning.

Guibert has agreed to give them Becket's martyrdom as part of the homily for tomorrow's Mass, and so we will honor his death as we say the Office for his feast, beginning with the eve and First Vespers this evening. Tomorrow at chapter I want to talk to them about Becket's earlier exile.

Originally I heard his story in drabs and pieces, burnished from passing through many hands; thoughts added, ambitions intruded. That Becket started out as skilled chancellor to Henry II, that he led his king's troops at the campaign at Toulouse—these spoke little more than loyalty in exchange for favoritism. When King Henry himself pushed through impediments and named Becket archbishop of Canterbury, it seemed simply an extension of his favored status, though we on the Continent caught our breath to realize Becket was the first in that office to have been native-born.

While we were buzzing about that, the unexpected took place on the British isle. The archbishop experienced a profound conversion, dramatic in its suddenness, a true turning of his love to God that, once started, only deepened with passing days. Henry did not weather the detachment.

> The souls of the just are in God's hands, beyond the reach of their tormentors' malice. Dead? Fools think so; think their end loss, their leaving us annihilation; but all is well with them. The world sees nothing but the pains they endure; they themselves have eyes only for what is immortal. So light their sufferings, so great the gain they win; God, all the while, did but test them, and testing them, found them worthy of Him. His

gold, tried in the crucible, His burnt-sacrifice, graciously accepted, they do but wait for the time of their deliverance. Then they will shine out, these just souls, unconquerable as the sparks that breathe out, now here, now there, among the stubble. Theirs to sit in judgement upon nations, to subdue whole peoples, under a Lord whose reign shall last for ever.[18]

January 6, 1179
Feast of the Epiphany

Now I find that most of us—myself included, to my great wonder—conceive of the Divine Office as music: absent the music, the precise ebb and flow of the melodies, the lines of the bare text are simply without substance. Arrowroot that blooms along the Rhine, uprooted and deprived of its watery element, withers and dies; just so are these words apparently imbedded in our memories via the melodies that house them. Unlike homilies and epistles, which are conceived solely for instructions, our antiphons, responsories, and hymns float in sound for the purpose of praise and thanksgiving. And as we sing, we are fed. The walls of our church are burnished with the sounds we breathe, the texts spiral higher. Unearthly light enters, we are bathed in it, because it is so moist and pungent, as with incense. We are washed, cleansed, and sing to greater purpose, clearer intention. Collectively we understand such presence, each to greater or lesser degree according to her gifts, generating the sound together like a body of sacred water drawn to bathe the delicate wings of an angel Wisdom, wings that unite heaven and earth.

Without sounding our praise, we are so many desiccated women. Our breathing is diminished; those of us who can even retrieve the dry word unsung, stumble through at different tempi. It is nearly impossible to finish together. Rhythms and cadences are lost to us. Anarchy. With no neumes described by the cantor's hand, real movement ceases. Doors do not open, and we are without purpose, whose days and nights were always swollen, so filled that all our moments were accountable! Silences once treasured as contemplative rests now stretch into awkward blanks as the time of Office is shortened by half without its music.

The only two busy, purposeful locations in our community are the scriptorium and the dispensary. The physical demands of illness and the copying of sacred words can still command our attention. Elsewhere, I see my women dispirited. Their bodies droop; hems drag along the floors as they move, outward signs that their physical health suffers. This is not the feverish kind of mortal illness that carried away my provosts. What moves among the sisters is more subtle. They cough often and breathe badly, complain of catarrh, poor digestion, melancholia, and generalized weakness. And now that clouds continually glower at us, blanketing the sun, despondency envelops our two houses. How can I reassure them that January days are now lengthening, when we have not glimpsed the sun at all these past four days?

I above all should not be dependent on visible proof for my hope, but it scours me, wears me away. I find myself looking for physical signs as if I were the simplest peasant.

Doing Christmas Matins without music was closer to rote performance than praise. The quality of our attention was dismal. When did it get so bad? We were well into late Advent when the real effects of the interdict began to be felt. At some point during that season we could no longer believe it was a simple mistake or misunderstanding that would be corrected with the exchange of a single letter. Each day our quota of light was shaved away; the number of black night hours continued to grow all the while the night office itself was markedly abbreviated by its loss of music. I then made the decision to allow the women extra sleep and instructed them to return to their cells after Matins. But extra sleep failed to refresh them. Many still complain of fatigue.

This morning when I called for the infirmarian's report, she told me that some are having difficulty falling asleep and ask for valerian regularly. Too many have access to substances whose properties and actions they barely understand. Almost all collecting of medicinal herbs is done now by lay sisters and a few women from the village, who share their knowledge with one another. My infirmarian points out that only those few choir nuns who have actually assisted her have any knowledge or appreciation of the powers of particular plants, used individually or in combination with others. After she left it occurred to me that this year's Lenten practice might consist of a thorough physical instruction for the whole community. They are so weary of texts and words. At least we can use real plants to instruct them. At this time of year plants are dried. Their colors are faded but recognizably different, one from the other. Besides, the distinctive shapes of leaves and seed heads are easily noted. Individual fragrances adhere even though muted.

I will instruct them myself, and those whose understanding extends to organization and classification can study further by using the written materials I long ago devised when we first came to Mount St. Rupert. Not all our more recent observations are recorded in the *Materia medica*,[19] and I fear that some of the knowledge will be lost with my death. I must rein in the urgency perpetually lurking about such thoughts. We now have the novices learning about medicinals by brewing the infusions and decoctions we require. I am well aware that there may be some overuse. The more important task for me this Lenten season is to reawaken their senses—so deadened without the regular practice of music—to the wonder of God's created world, the bounty designed for our praise. It is impossible this year to wait for the promise of Easter and the greening of spring. I feel they will be too late.

In truth the waiting is exhausting for all of us. It is beyond patience and robs us of our duty and joy like the worst thievery. I am certain it is God's will that our music be restored to us, and I have been absolutely obedient to that truth as it has been revealed to me in divine visions.

The true vision urges me to a reasoned argument that I will send to Mainz in the form of a letter. Our archbishop cares not for the testimony of heart or soul. He will have careful reasoning, prose with parallel construction and any other rhetorical devices I can recall from Volmar's suggestions over the years. Not only will he and his prelates be made to understand the theological power of music for the order of monastics: it will be clear and unmistakable that our two opposing sides mark the division between good and evil, and that all of their actions place them in league with the devil. I doubt it can be done quickly, but I sense it is a necessity for our release from bondage.

January 21, 1179
Feast of St. Agnes, Virgin and Martyr

My inclination might have been to start from our present situation, but Guibert encourages building my argument from the beginning. He has not tired in four days of continuous dictation, and I go back once more to think, rethink, and revise the opening sections. Above all, I would have the minions of the archbishop understand that divine authority is the ground of all being, and that there are only two possible courses of action in any decision: one is for good, the other for evil.

> To the Prelates of Mainz:
>
> In a vision that even before I was born was imprinted on me by the Artisan God, I was forced to write this, bound as we are now to our superiors, because a man who died was, at the behest of his priest, buried among us in good faith. When, a few days after the burial, we were ordered by our superiors to expel him from our cemetery, I was seized by no little terror and therefore looked to the true light as is my practice. And with my eyes open, I saw in my soul that if the man's body were exposed, we would by expelling him in this way threaten our home with vast danger of a terrible blackness, an envelopment by the kind of dense cloud that precedes tempests and thunderstorms.
>
> Therefore we could neither take it upon ourselves to expel the body of the dead man, insofar as he was confessed and communicated and buried without contradiction, nor acquiesce in the judgment you in

haste urged or ordered: and not at all to make light of the judgment of honorable men or of the command of our prelates, but so we would not seem to be barbarous women violating the sacraments of Christ, with which the man was protected while still alive. Nevertheless, in order not to live entirely as disobedients, we have thus far abstained from singing our canticles of divine praise, in accord with the interdict, and from partaking of the body of the Lord, which we were accustomed to receive regularly each month.

A careful beginning to set the scene, but only the smallest part of it. For the argument itself, I begin at the beginning with Adam, who before the expulsion from the Garden could both hear and produce every conceivable sound, even the music of the spheres—the whole gamut of sounds audible and singable. The argument itself is centered on Psalm 150.

I heard a voice proceeding from the living light concerning all diversity of praise, as when David in the Psalms said, "Praise Him with sound of trumpet, praise Him with psaltery and harp. Praise Him with timbrel and choir, praise Him with strings and organ. Praise Him on resounding cymbals: praise Him on cymbals of joy: let every spirit praise the Lord. Alleluia." In these words we are instructed through exterior things about interior things—how, according to the formed, material qualities of musical instruments, we ought to convert and inform our human interior by our Offices, most especially through our praises of the Creator. To these things we diligently turn our attention and recall how mankind searched for the voice of the living spirit that Adam lost through disobedience, though while still innocent before the transgression he had no little fellowship with the praise-sounds of angels, which they possess from their spiritual nature, from the spirit that is God. He lost the sympathy with angelic voices he had had in Paradise. And he lost the knowledge with which he had been endowed before his transgression. It was as if he fell asleep, then wakened to dream about those things he had seen while sleeping; rendered ignorant and uneasy, he was deceived by a suggestion from the devil, and for opposing the Creator's will became entangled in the interior dark of ignorance, a punishment for iniquity. Yet it is fact that God reserves for original blessedness those souls chosen by the light of truth, and to this end devised a plan to refresh them, to fill their hearts as much as possible with an infusion of the prophetic spirit so they would be restored in the interior illumination Adam had before his justly punished fault.

And since they were being recalled by God to His sweetness and praise, which Adam enjoyed before he fell but could not recollect in his exile, the holy prophets, infused with the Holy Spirit through that divine sense they had received, were taught not only psalms and canticles whose singing influences devotion through listening, but taught as well divers instruments of musical art by which a world of sounds is brought forth: thus the prophets composed as much from the shapes and qualities of the instruments as from a sense of the words' singing, so with right mind and practice we might be instructed about interior things. Those earnest and wise to imitate the holy prophets invented several kinds of *organa* through which they might sing in accord with the delight in their souls, and these they sang and communicated by a signaling with sections of their fingers (separated by their bendings at the joints), a sweet recalling that Adam was formed by the finger of God, which is the Holy Spirit—Adam, whose voice failed in the sounding of harmony and in all musical arts and, if it had remained in its original state, could by no means have carried its virtue and sonority to the weaknesses of mortal men, o sweet fault! Now when Adam's deceiver, the devil, heard that humankind had begun to sing by the inspiration of God and could, through this, be summoned to the recollection of the sweetness of the fatherland's celestial songs, his engines of cleverness seemed ineffectual, and he was so terrified and tortured that he had his hands full to contrive and investigate one after another mulifarious prescription for evil. And he does not desist from destroying the confession and beauty of divine praise, not only from the heart of a human being, through evil suggestions of unclean thoughts or various possessions, but also from the heart of the Church, wherever he is able through disagreements and scandals and unjustly acquired oppressions. That is why you and all prelates have your hands full and must thoroughly and with the greatest vigilance air the causes for which you would by hurtful interdict close the mouth of any church singing the praise of God or cripple its members by suspending their sacraments.

And diligently take pains that such a judgment be out of zeal for God's justice; moved neither by indignation nor wrongful emotion of the soul, do not be dragged along by any ulterior motive, always on guard lest in judging you be set upon by Satan, he who dragged humanity from celestial harmony and paradisal delight. Consider well, therefore: as the body of Jesus Christ was born from the Holy Spirit and the holiness of the Virgin Mary, even so the canticles of praise stemming from celestial harmonies have through that Spirit found their home in the Church. Truly the body is the garment of the soul, which has a living voice, and therefore it is fitting that the body with soul sing through its voice the praises of God, and that the spirit of prophecy order through this signifying union that God be praised in cymbals of jubilation and the music of the many instruments that wise and earnest people invented, for all that pertains to useful and necessary human art was found through the breath God released into the body of man: therefore it is just that in all things God be praised. When we listen to singing we frequently breathe and sigh, instructed in the nature of the soul and the celestial harmonies; thus the spirit of the prophet David, deeply considering and knowing spiritual nature (how soul moves in sympathy with sound), exhorts us in a psalm to sing the psalms confessing God with lute, psaltery, and harp—the lute that rounds to the higher tones, towards the *intentio* of the spirit; the ten-stringed harp in its desire to restore us to the contemplation of the law. They then who would without weighing the absolute truth of reason impose silence on the Church in its singing of God's praise, shall lack the company of angelic praise in heaven; who have unjustly plundered on earth the honor of His praise can amend solely through true penitence and humble reparation! They then who hold the keys to heaven, let them guard strictly neither to open those things that should be closed nor to close those that should be open, because harshest judgment will fall on those who rule without the solicitude required by the Apostle. And I heard a voice saying "Who created heaven?—God. Who is like unto that?—No one. You

> faithful, offer no resistance to God, nor oppose Him: do not submerge your fortitude, but let Him protect you in His justice. These are womanish times, for God's justice among men is wanting. Now let fortitude bud forth the justice of God, and the woman-turned-warrior live on against injustice till she completely rout God's enemies![20]

It is my finest sermon, and I wonder at the alarming length of it. Exhaustion that signals the worst pain and weakness threatens to carry me off. Dear Lord, if it be now, before we are restored to our rightful music making and I am not to see our vindication, I have at least spoken the truth as it has been revealed to me, and it has been recorded. Those who come after me cannot be ignorant of it: music is the bridge to life before the Fall, and to life beyond.

February 2, 1179
Purification of the Virgin, Candlemas

It is well before Lauds; there is time to tell you that last night I dreamed we were measuring the gardens and the orchard. You looked a bit ghostly, but strong. By ghostly, I mean only that there was a translucence to your complexion. Also your features were slightly fluid; that is, they arranged and rearranged themselves as we spoke, so that as a result your expression shifted: from tenderness, through determination, even outrage, each of many qualities I know in you over these seventy-some years.

Did I say we were both younger, as well? For I also saw myself, as you might see me, in a watery mirror. As we moved among the raised beds with measuring rods, I noted how your feet barely touched the earth. You seemed to be floating, unmarked by the muddy earth pulling at my dirty overshoes. When I remarked about it, you smiled in your particularly encouraging manner and reassured me that there was a definite limit to the impedimenta of old age—that at some point moving ceases being one of the chief difficulties.

I smiled wryly in return, asking that you note clearly how I was still managing to walk on my own (which is of course not true, but so it was in the dream). You were not impressed, and we got on with our measuring of gardens. You'll remember how the gardens are laid out these days—the medicinals in neat parallel rows, the kitchen garden partially shaded by the overhang of the refectory, and the best of the flower gardens placed close enough to the church to perfume it summer evenings at Vespers and Compline. They are basically all rectangular beds and so easy enough to measure by walking their length and width.

In the dream, the raised beds were nearly that way to begin with, then radically transformed as we moved among them. Stopping at the first bed of artemesias, you suggested to me that I use my staff to draw them into the shape of a large initial. I was not puzzled at all. Drawing myself up to full height and without even a trace of the tremor I have struggled with for the last several years, using the wax tablet, I traced a T with a flourish and watched joyfully as the plants artfully arranged themselves into that shape.

After I had repeated the gesture with many other capitals, you suggested I decorate them as if they were initials in our Book of Life. Those were your words, "our Book of Life," as if this were something I should know well, something we'd been working on together for some period of time. From here on, the initials became more ornate and fantastical—blossoms of myriad shades with vegetables forming interlacings of green. Imagine rubricating in green, rather than red!

Next the beds took on several dimensions: some of the letters rose into the air, so that words could be read on one flat plane, or alternately on several vertical planes, forming acrostic patterns of a mystical nature; I'd call them cryptic, except they were all so ornate.

I suppose it was the messages and symbolic meanings that were cryptic. Viewing the letters and words from above, as if seeing one vast page, I saw a stark cross emerge as part of the complex pattern. When you understood that I had seen the shape of the cross clearly, you suggested we move on to the orchard-cemetery. I was reluctant, for fear that our awe and appreciation were necessary for the continuity of the mystery. You remarked with a curious levity how uncharacteristic reluctance was for your dearest friend the abbess.

Just as you said that, I heard the trees of the orchard bursting into leaf. It was abrupt and dramatic, and drew both of us down into the cemetery, the leaves snapping into their full shapes the way fans are unfurled with sudden, meaningful gestures. I awakened to hear the snaps turn into brusque knocking at the door of my cell.

It was sister infirmarian, who says I have been delirious and with fever since my return from Mainz. I remember nothing of the return. I might have frozen for all I knew, but that Guibert had wrapped me in blankets of bear and fox. I barely remember offering prayers at the chapel of St. Gothard upon our arrival, or the overbearing splendor of the archiepiscopal palace itself. I am told I pleaded our case with eloquence, that the prelates were astonished at the contents of the letter. But I found them unmoving, and am not ashamed when my prioress tells me I returned home full of tears. I prefer dream to delirium, liturgy and movement to enforced silence. If being conscious and awake robs me of all nourishment and comfort, I care little for recovery.

February 14, 1179
Ash Wednesday

It must be two weeks since our return from Mainz. Of the first I remember nothing at all. Like some ancient animal, I must have been hibernating the winter. Or like an insect in a cocoon, body encrusted in tight wrappings to keep the cries and thoughts from flying to the four winds. But my spirit lives; wrapping cloths that could have been shroud unwind.

Sometime during the same interval, my prioress requests an audience. It is urgent. She reminds me that Lent approaches, and she begs me to consider that we all dress in sackcloth and ashes for the forty days and nights, that we all become public penitents in our own house and thereby justify our cause, plead our case. My vision clarifies, and I can once more focus. In the Shadow of the Living Light it is clear we must pray for the soul of our reconciled young man and for the life of our community. We must pray that the shackles fall from the eyes of our archbishop and his prelates. But we will not go in sackcloth and ashes. Only for today will the beautiful brows of my loyal women be painted with burnt palms from our Lord's triumphant entry into Jerusalem, and I am strong enough to lead the flock at the Introit. If we cannot sing the words of Sapientia, we will say it on high, and together, our lips and breathing in unified movement:

> There is nothing, Lord, but claims thy pity;
> thou hatest nothing that thou hast made. When men
> repent thou dost overlook their sins and pardon them;
> art thou not the Lord, our own God?[21]

Why then, if our Lord Himself pardons the repentant sinner, do the lords of this world, worldly archbishops and their minions, set themselves over and above His judgment? How can they refuse to pardon one who was clearly reconciled before his death? And I shudder at the knowledge of how their refusal is capable of distorting, even perverting this penitential season for my women. Already seven have cried to me privately that our obedience feels more to them like punishment, and the forty days and nights of Lent have just begun.

The deeply hopeful text of the proper chant at Communion cries out to be sung, to strengthen our stalwartness through the familiar words of the first psalm: "Whose heart is set on the law of the Lord, day and night, shall yield fruit when the season comes."[22] Yet we can neither raise our voices in song nor partake of the elements of Communion this Ash Wednesday. How are we to endure without body, blood, or voice through a Lenten season?

I wonder sometimes whether this great trial is in itself what keeps me alive. My visions have been clear. The will of God is manifest through the Voice of Wisdom. My actions have been impeccable. And yet I approach the eighty-first year of a life filled with illness and trials, determined to overcome the sentence that has been unjustly placed upon us as if my life were inexhaustible. Somewhere is the possibility that I neglect preparation for my own death in the face of what presents itself as the most difficult battle of my life. Hiding in some corner of my being must be agony and even outrage at being asked to approach the table of my death without eating and drinking what has been my lifelong sustenance, the assurance of His flesh in my flesh, the melting into the limbs that have formed my lifelong embrace.

The confusion is numbing. Too much reasoning

causes the mystery to escape. There is surely a way in which this approach to his resurrection can also be preparation for my own death, a way of understanding it as a coming, like Advent—the assurance that all my desperate skirmishes with evil in the world have not been ends in themselves but, rather, shapers of the soul I prepare for my Beloved. Let me be certain our voices will be restored through such preparation:

> Let the priests that wait upon the Lord make their lament between porch and altar, crying, Spare the people, Lord, spare them: do not silence, Lord, the lips that sing thy praise.[23]

February 18, 1179
First Sunday in Lent

I wonder if it is only my imagination that begins to see our community as one piece of that much larger puzzle involving powerful players from both Church and state. The powers that entangle us were just those I had hoped to place in abeyance when, some fifteen years ago, the emperor awarded Rupertsberg a charter of protection in perpetuity. I thought the charter would strengthen a wall of protection for us against the machinery of worldly politics. Yet it was around the same time that sacred and secular authority became, alternately, ever more sharply pitted against one another or hopelessly entwined in nearly all of Western Christendom.

Christ's teaching, "Render therefore to Caesar the things that are Caesar's, and to God the things that are God's," seemed to express with perfect economy the intentions of the earliest Christians. Certainly not in our times. For example, we flounder in a morass deepened by the papal schism that went on in our Church for nearly twenty years. The schism is finally resolved and His Holiness Alexander rightfully returned to the throne of St. Peter in Rome, but so much of what was lost over those many years cannot be restored. Nearly all the powerful players are out of order, quite literally misplaced in location, office, duties, and powers.

Even before the schism, the stage was set when our German Frederick Barbarossa was elevated from king to emperor. As with the ancient Roman emperors, Frederick's temporal limits began to melt. Perhaps I should have drawn the comparison with Caesar when I wrote to him, but the figure that came to me in the Shadow of the Living Light all those years ago was Nebuchadnezzar, and I forwarded my warning to the emperor in strong language from our fledgling community.

Emperor Frederick took it upon himself to initiate the election of three different antipopes, then replaced our own archbishop of Mainz with that worldly linguist and scholar misnamed Christian, who now holds us in thrall. Unlike St. Thomas of Canterbury, Christian did not resign as chancellor to the emperor when elevated to archbishop. Instead, Archbishop Christian proved himself a great military strategist for his emperor, fought for years in Italy as commander of his troops, and now, with the fighting ended, acts as the emperor's chief officer in negotiating a settlement as favorable to the emperor as possible. And though the peace is finally signed, the archbishop is still absent from our soil, not available to God's truth, which we in all humility firmly uphold in our house.

How sure-footed I feel I have been, how carefully I have chosen the true path, watched for the light, listened for the Voice of Wisdom. How could all have heated to such a punishing boil that now, in the calm of a settlement both in the papacy and among powerful clerics and kings, we ourselves are still forbidden to sing the Divine Office—our daily life's blood?

Dear friend, right now I long for the comfort of our fine conversation, your devoted ear and moral goodness. Even without outward music, I pray for you daily and sense that you hear me. To some degree my life's work depended upon you for as long as I can remember, and does so still. The gentleness of your death, the way each so-gradual diminishment in physical powers was balanced by ever sharpening spiritual emotions, lulled me into some paltry judgment that you would always be there. So for the years immediately following your death, your physical replacement was my preoccupation: finding a suitable provost for our community, secretary and scribe for myself.

Wondrous to me now, how little I thought about the whole picture, unable to look beyond my preoccupation to see what larger forces might have been disrupted by my search. It was simply a setback when an answer came from Disibodenberg that Abbot Helengerus refused our request and would not provide a provost to serve our community. I thought we had fought and won that battle at least twenty years before with Abbot Kuno, who at first would not allow you to accompany us to establish St. Rupertsberg. Kuno was an abbot jealous of our threatened autonomy, perhaps even righteously fearful that we as women would not survive without physical protection from the male monastery. It was probably your own unquestioning loyalty to me that tipped the balance in that controversy. Neither Abbot Kuno nor many of the monks were pleased with the outcome, and it was several years before our rift was healed, as we continued to quibble about my women's dowries. Kuno later surprised me by requesting some songs in honor of St. Disibode, patron saint of the old community, and I was pleased to fulfill the request. Since that time some twenty years have passed, and I had assumed we were in relative amity with St. Disibode's and its new abbot, Helengerus.

When, at your death, Abbot Helengerus refused our request, I was shocked; however, knowing the man's reputation for being troublesome and inconstant, I turned quickly to higher authority and wrote directly to His Holiness Alexander, whose office as true pope I had supported through all the years of treachery. In all humility, I reminded him of the biblical precedents for rewarding penitent petitioners:

> Now O gentlest father, my sisters and I bend our knees before your paternal piety, praying that you deign to regard the poverty of this poor little woman. We are in great distress because the abbot of Mount St. Disibod and his brothers have taken away our privileges and the right of election which we have always had, rights which we have been ever careful to retain. For if they will not grant us reverential and religious men, such as we seek, spiritual religion will be totally destroyed among us. Therefore, my lord, for God's sake, help us, so that we may retain the man we have elected to that office. Or, if not, let us seek out and receive others, where we can, who will look after us in accordance with the will of God and our own needs. . . .[24]

His Holiness was entirely sympathetic to our needs; nevertheless, the office was not filled quickly. It took nearly a year before the negotiations were completed, Pope Alexander having written to my dear nephew Wezelin, then provost at St. Andrea's in Cologne, instructing him to come to our aid. Wezelin then persuaded Helengerus to fulfill our agreement, and finally Godfrey arrived. His time with us was brief, for he was taken suddenly by fever before a full year had passed. In that short time the poor man was preoccupied with a mandate he had received to undertake my *vita*. He interviewed me many times as to the nature of my visions, whether they had started when I was a child or in adulthood, how and under what circumstances I saw them. And did it also become something of a preoccupation of my own?

No matter, for the *vita* was abandoned at Godfrey's

death. Guibert shows interest in reviving the project, but nothing distracts me now from having the interdict removed; at my death, it may be that my life must be its own confession and spiritual biography. "By your fruits . . ."

Dear friend, my mind sometimes wanders off. My intention was to discuss with you the possibility that some action of mine initiated in the past created an opening just large enough for the devil to insinuate himself, for the interdict is a matter with evil at its core. No rational intelligence stands as its cause or cure. Nor will the gift of understanding untangle its bonds. For months I thought otherwise. I appealed with rational intelligence for the man interred in our sacred orchard. I turned to the authority of Wisdom in order to justify my obedience to a higher power. Even the sound theological argument I painstakingly developed to persuade the prelates at Mainz fell on deaf ears and instead had the primary effect of deepening my own understanding of the salivific power of music for all time. But, again, I wander from the possibility that I may have unwittingly threatened powerful forces.

I see now how my unguarded appeal to the true pope those several years ago, and his response to me, may have stirred up the force of the devil and unleashed the wrath of Emperor Barbarossa; his clever chancellor, our archbishop Christian; and his prelates at Mainz. (I will not even consider the wavering Helengerus—that is an old and well-known story to you; as you are fully aware, he is practically without enough stability even to lead his own community.) I could not see any of this four years ago, when I turned to His Holiness for assistance in obtaining a provost to replace you. God only knows how I was bereft at your death, orphaned again as I was that one other time with the double loss of Rikkarda. Never before your death had I been left to fuss with the final details of the setting down of my visions. Not only that. More subtle considerations were suddenly at sea: the way you had of reassuring me that what I had received from the Voice of Wisdom, though it may have been strange, was truly of God and therefore to be given voice for understanding by the people of God. I see now that I never quite gave up needing that reassurance, but it was not until your leaving that I was even aware of it.

I know what you will say, that in the end I was able to turn for help to my old friend in Christ, Abbot Ludwig of St. Eucharius, for his scribal approval of the last book of visions, but it was not the same. Nor is he in any position to help or even understand our position regarding the burial of a young man in our sacred ground. How could we have imagined an interdict for our pains? What could you say to the icy strangulation of our voices, the barrenness that inflicts the spacious interior of our church? Only your death could have so much further schooled me in loneliness as to bear this long loss of singing with the angels.

February 25, 1179
Second Sunday in Lent

It is reported to me once again that people are waiting, they expect something from me. It is now so-and-so many years since you have written down your visions, they say. Only a few people are chosen to benefit from your wisdom any more, through individual letters inspired by the Shadow of the Living Light. Such clamor is brought to me by my diligent secretary-scribe, our provost Guibert. People say even more. Rumor has it that you have lost the gift of prophecy; furthermore, that the interdict itself is a sign of that loss. It indicates a dramatic loss of power. Where now is that fiery potency that prevails over all, sees as an eagle sees, flies above the dross that pulls on the rest of humanity, dashing it down?

O stulti! How little they understand, my true friend in Christ. What do they really know of life in the fiery furnace? Should we even attempt to tell them how it is possible that I am so old now, so exhausted, but the furnace is inexhaustible? It warms me; it burns me even, has burned me often with such sacred wounds. I wonder myself at such a mystery: what was at my earliest perception something of awe bordering on terror, so strange and foreign to me as a bare whip of a sapling, without leaves, without training or development, lately becomes nearly my own element. Finally, I am more of it than it of me.

But this is never amenable to words of reason, only of poetry, parable, and music. For it is clear enough to the mind of men that there are four elements, that some creatures live in water and they are the fishes and mammoths of the sea. Some creatures are of the air which are birds, insects, and fowl. Many more even live on the earth—all the animals, the trees and grasses, plants and people, male and female. Some even move in more than one element, requiring both earth and air, even earth, air, and water continuously together for their being.

What can they understand about living more and more in the element of fire?

I too am not without fears, my dear Volmar, as you have always known, but they are not what other people think they are. I too acknowledge my vast age, shriveled limbs, turned-in cheeks, and stiff-slithering gait. In fact, I wonder at it. But I am not without the strength that has been my life. In fact, the more I am a husk, the more easily it is enlivened, as audible to my senses as the wind blowing through a field of ripened grain. And just as simply, for I am more and more of it, less and less of myself. The fiery element is of great power and mystery that is its own, and it would be a great lie to imagine that I had any control of it.

It moves powerfully and mysteriously, just as it will, and although I have devoted the better part of my life to fearing, then approaching, befriending, respecting, and loving it, it is not mine. Its beauty is now far, far greater than I could ever have imagined, and it only grows more difficult each day to live anywhere else for any human purpose whatsoever. You who were always better anchored to the element of earth, then buried in it and become its deep agent, know this best. Without you, I took a sudden burning leap at your death. Now I can only do what it chooses, can only live as long as it moves me, can only resume singing out loud to the heavens the liquid light of the Divine Office if it pleases.

March 4, 1179
Third Sunday in Lent

The weather is hideous—colorless and frigid, no smells or sounds. We long ago blanketed all of our gardens in hay, and it is far too early to unearth them for planting. The earth is gone to gray, trees ravaged skeletons of themselves, birds silenced. The last two mornings even the water for drinking has frozen and must be thawed. My women are bitter and with reason. We too are silenced, and my senses thirst. I long to die—but in spring or fall—never in this wasting time. I need to be buried truly in earth, my body gently received, pillowed in fragrant loam, wild seedlings the birds and trees have wantonly dropped pushing up between my toes, eager roots encircling my bony fingers like green rings. Or in the fall, my body adding to the winey smell of rotting leaves, sharp-angled sun shaving rock surfaces and bird wings high above me with slices of color.

I long for such a rich death. These past four months have been a purgatory, its stunning details unimagined before they were upon me, each reversal producing yet another misfortune, nearly like midwifing one monster birth after another. I marvel today what evil snare prompted me to organize the facts and proofs according to their satisfaction, as if we were so many begging litigants rather than a community of dedicated virgins.

For weeks I worked out yet another plan, lined up my most powerful allies to pursue justice for an action we had taken that required no justification whatsoever. It was a simple feat of detection to locate the honorable knight who had sought absolution at the same time as the young man we so innocently buried in our midst. The obliging knight visited here, spoke with me, and provided the name of the priest who reconciled them both. I myself then wrote to the priest, who in turn accompanied the knight for an audience with our influential friend Philip, archbishop of Cologne. Philip received them sympathetically: when they had pleaded their cause, he understood its truth and how it related to our own painful situation.

And finally Archbishop Philip added his own authority to their argument, so that ultimately they arranged that all three honorable men—priest, knight, and archbishop—would present the case to the clerics in Mainz who presided over Archbishop Christian's perennial neglect. God knows such elaborately organized proofs should never have been required. Moral rectitude has always been with us. My visions have been clear and consistent from the first.

But human proofs are required for the powers who sit *in cathedra,* even when they absent their religious duties and sit on foreign soil. I myself have finally admitted to physical limitations. I could not take my body again to the archiepiscopal palace in Mainz and must await their report.

March 11, 1179
Fourth Sunday in Lent

Archbishop Philip's judgment was sufficient to convince the prelates of Mainz, who assumed their own archbishop would concur. So briefly our throats moistened with music flowing heavenward in praise of God, but for how long? Has it been two days yet? Or was it ten? No matter. Christian cancels Philip's reprieve for us. Resumption of our very life's work is stalled, with Holy Week nearly upon us. The world withers without the sound of sung praise, our reprieve denied. No sooner have I found and forged one link in the chain that would renew our consecrated lives than another link breaks.

Time becomes our fiercest enemy. How can my beloved music's chief element be such a driving scourge? Music obeys laws of time that are forever filled with mystery and in which we fully participate over and over again; yet music itself is of a larger order, one that is beyond even time. We humans are music's agency but not its source. God's will is similarly beyond my grasp. Its timing is surely not mine, and I can only pray to be its living agent, its willing servant, begging aloud in a demand for righteousness.

How little the clerics of Mainz have cared for such depths. I doubt they even sing the Office at the cathedral, busy as they are adjudicating cases, managing lands, and administering the business of the diocese. Over many years they applauded my visions and appreciated their beauty so long as it had nothing to do with the world in which they themselves moved. Even our disagreement over the schism and restoration of Alexander to the papacy has been for them simply an issue of politics, its outcome dependent upon enlisting the largest number of influential parties, managing to be on the winning side when the outcome was finally declared, and negotiating skillfully with plenty of resources to bargain if—as it seems after fifteen years of struggle—the rightful man was returned to office. For our many German supporters of the three antipopes set up to oppose Alexander, little or nothing of the struggle has concerned itself with truth.

I have not allowed any decision, any action that I can think of to be dictated by fear. Yet, the fickle aimlessness, the lack of consistency of power in the world is dizzying. The same emperor who granted our immunity, three times refused to support Alexander, our true pope. Not two years after granting our immunity, the same emperor deposed our worthy archbishop of Mainz, Conrad of Wittelsbach, and put in his place a man of much lesser nobility, with the unlikely name of Christian. Archbishop Christian has proved himself brilliant in the world, absent in spirit. His mind and wit are like sharp arrows; in addition to Latin, he is fluent in five different tongues. He is a consummate politician, has served Barbarossa's interests brilliantly in Italy, where he has resided almost entirely over the last five or six years. To young clerics in Mainz his word is law, his person unknown. Imperial Italy flourishes, while lands of the archbishopric here are mortgaged and the see of Mainz grows deeper in debt.

This Christian, warming his wintry bones in Italy, renews the terms of the interdict. And pierced my heart, but not my spirit. I am much too old to worry about losing my life, and I will not have my women witness their abbess yielding to such deceitful play of power at the end. I will not humiliate myself nor my staunch supporters by dragging these old bones through the snow to beg for yet another audience. Our archbishop cares not for the testimony of heart or soul, but he will not be spared words through my pen. He will receive one more letter from me.

March 18, 1179
Passion Sunday

Strangely, though I had worked in fits and starts for weeks on my long letter to the prelates of Mainz, the letter to Archbishop Christian in Italy nearly wrote itself. I think it cannot be faulted for lack of propriety to office, nor is the mandate demanded by the divine voice of my vision in any way betrayed.

The focus of the letter to Christian is at once broad landscape plus particular, chronological details. Once more I recapitulated for his perusal each step in the drama that has ensnared us, its dizzying twistings and turnings in the face of our unyielding innocence and obedience to truth. It is necessary that he know how like the unexpected return of a hurricane came the news that he had contravened the lifting of the interdict, how it battered against my women already so wounded from months of being deprived of our sacred song. One may not assume the power of a whirlwind without taking the responsibility for its possible destructiveness.

> Even though, most gracious lord, we should have had the greatest trust in your mercy, we received from the Mainz prelates after your return from the synod in Rome a letter of your interdict of divine services. I am confident that had you known the truth of this matter, you in your fatherly love would never have sent such. Because of this ruling, most gentle father, we now find ourselves suffering much greater pain and grief than we had under the prior ruling. Finally, in the vision of my

> soul whose words you have never doubted, I was ordered to speak from mind and heart, since "it is better for me to fall into the hands of men than to forsake the command of my God." And so, most gracious lord, I beseech you in the love of the Holy Spirit: respectful of the Father who is eternal, who sent His Word of tenderest greening power into the womb of the Virgin for the salvation of humankind, do not choose to disdain the tears of your sorrowing daughters who, from fear of God, bear the misery and anguish of an unjust letter. Let the Holy Spirit fill you so you have mercy upon us, even as you yourself will long for this mercy at the end of your life.[25]

A fair copy was sent off late this morning, and a remarkable calm pervades me at last. Either a most clement and peaceful death approaches with unlooked-for gentleness, or this is premonitory assurance that we will yet participate in the mystery of Christ's death and resurrection with sacred song and blessed blood.

It seems certain that this time we will be vindicated. Our highly schooled archbishop will not fail to hear the voice of Susanna in the letter, adding the vigor of beauteous youth to my decrepitude. For was she not beset by the snares of reputable men backed by a whole community blinded to innocent truth by vested power? With what joy would we end our unjust siege as that wonderful story of Daniel ends: "All the assembly cried out with a loud voice, and they blessed God, who saves those who trust in him."

March 31, 1179
Paschal Vigil

And now that we at last are free,

> Let us sing to the Lord, for He is gloriously magnified:
> horse and rider He hath thrown into the sea;
> He is become my helper and protector unto salvation.
> V. He is my God, and I will glorify Him:
> the God of my father, and I will exalt Him.
> V. The Lord destroys warfare:
> the Lord is His name.[26]

Part Three

April 8, 1179
First Sunday after Easter

The evil unleashed upon us was finally remanded at nearly the last possible moment. (How to approach the last days of Christ's life in absolute silence was beyond even my imagining.) Archbishop Christian's letter of reprieve arrived from Rome, and I read most of it to them in refectory the same day.[27] Less than two days later came Holy Week, our sounds escaping everywhere, whether in joy or wailing with Our Lord. So much sound, so much energy and movement, it was as if we were all nesting birds like the ones building furiously now in our orchard, as if we might all have bits of twine, twigs, and grasses dripping from our mouths as we flapped about!

After so many months of being silenced, we are all highly sensitized to timbre, range, and reverberation in the particular container that is our church. I think the great beauty of the two days of end-to-end rehearsals we had to prepare for the Triduum was due to the quality of *listening* on the part of everyone. So much listening was a great gain out of our suffering. And not just outer listening. Wilhelmina, for example, has really learned to attend to her inner voice; I can see in her eyes that it continues.

No doubt when the joy of this suddenly sound-charged jubilation dissipates, Wilhelmina, like me, will have to struggle with discrepancies between inner and outer sound. When the inner sound of a particularly well-conceived piece of music reaches greater perfection than the outer performance, dissatisfaction with human limitations can be a plague for me, and even now I consciously curb its demands.

For some of my women, the rewards of emerging from the long silence are less subtle; many have confessed the simple relief of having to be bound by outer constraints. I know the more timid among them, and those who before coming to our community spent years in obedience to the good opinion of society, were greatly torn by my consistent decisions and actions during the fracture with Mainz. It amazes me still that they were all nonetheless loyal; in spite of all my efforts to teach them, many cannot discern between inner and outer authority. From beginning to end, they never truly understood that I was obedient only to God, and that desecrating the peace of that Christian body in our cemetery would have been a desecration of that obedience. For those women—loyal but confused—the conflict they feel between the will of God and that of powerful authority in the world is paralyzing. It turns quickly into experience of fear, which always mutes the true voice of Love.

I was surprised to discover that my own singing voice had almost entirely withdrawn during this interval of the interdict. It is of little importance. It took me by surprise, but hardly matters to the health of the community. For several years I have had three women who cantor so beautifully, it is a joy for me to hear the differences of tempo and timbre among them. Each one's voice is so distinctive that simply intoning the incipit elicits a response from the choir of a distinctly different sound. From long before the interdict was imposed, my role in choir has been more like the figurehead of our ship. The sound of the abbatial staff commands absolute authority, as do the directions of my hand, but these are the results of long training. My energy is increasingly elsewhere.

Still, it was a matter of some wonder to me, during our great rebirth of sound for Holy Week, that my own singing came in such fits and starts. I recalled the many years and decades when Volmar and I shared the burden of those passion-filled weeks—the lamentations I wailed, the Passions he chanted.

Guibert did a creditable job. He is energetic and devoted; at the same time, he is content to have a young deacon assisting at all times, who then naturally sings the Exultet at the vigil and helps distribute the load more equitably. But you, my dearest friend, until you were taken with that sudden last fever, your voice was strong and persuasive, and I recall you even persuaded me not to allow another priest, or even a deacon, to assist you until you were already bedridden. You and I did it all, even at Holy Week some years: did too much, I suppose; but the perfection we sought was matchless, and the intimacy of our souls an offering of exceptional beauty.

It is hard to describe how the breath in my belly is still sufficient; I checked with my hand to see that inspiration was yet considerable, if no longer vigorous, certainly enough to sustain the tones. It must be that the inspirited breath is going elsewhere, supporting some other species of sound. Perhaps you heard it?

Later

Dearest friend, I must have dozed after writing in my journal. It happens so often now, but this time I finally heard you. My own head, face forward, very frontal appeared, but larger than life and old as Abraham, as I these days often feel. Grizzled hair billows unruly from under my veil. A small cloud of buff-colored substance rolls out of my mouth as I speak words that melt into this substance, not heard, but subsumed into the liquid shape. Next, the cloud of substance, still growing, is no longer opaque. It begins to obscure and finally replace the part of my head and face it drifts in front of. My heart beats too rapidly. As it races in fear of disappearance, your kind and familiar voice—though with quite a resounding gong in it—says, "Domina, this is the best part."

April 15, 1179
Second Sunday after Easter

My dear Volmar, your appeared last night in my dream once more. Perhaps you know that already, for you were so vivid it was more like a visit than an appearance—the perfecting of our Easter joy to find you at work beside me.

In the dream we were industrious as always. You looked fresh and rested, eager to the task. Your tonsure was typically ragged but full, and the blue sky reflected on your bent head signaled the fact that we were outdoors. Together we sang the hymn for Lauds, *Aurora lucis rutilat.*

> Dawn browns the sky,
> air resounds it praises,
> earth triumphs
> and hell shudders
>
> as the powerful Lord
> draws out our ancestors
> from morbid chains
> to the light of life.
>
> Past guards, bonds and roofs
> this victor rises
> who buries death
> in his own grave.[28]

We sang as we watched spring advance; it progressed moment by moment rather than day by day. As I raised my eyes and looked around, I marveled at how my old eyes were sharpened in your presence. Details of our rugged landscape as it drops to the river in the distance have become blurred to my eyes in the last dozen years, not to speak of threads and letters held too close. Now every beloved detail came forward in its round separateness, at the same time perfectly fitted into the whole.

The way spring arrived was remarkable. Flocks of particular kinds of birds materialized in the form of distinctively shaped clouds. Judging from the color, I think the first group were orioles; and no sooner had all the bright-feathered birds lighted on the bare branches of what seemed a winter-dormant cherry tree than green leaves sprouted on every branch, along with sprays of pale pink blossoms. Seconds later fully ripe garnet-colored cherries hung from the same branches. It was like Aaron's rod magically flourishing in flower, fruit, and leaf simultaneously signaled by the feathered touch of the orange-winged orioles.

Such a brilliant succession of events continued with lovely rhythmic explosions as each cloud materialized. As I recall, the next group of birds were turtle doves that roosted on an apple tree, then purple finches on a pear, nightingales on a quince, and so on until every tree was adorned with the total sum of its characteristic beauty and fruit. You can imagine the heady smell—the moist greening of spring plus the combined odors of the various fruit blossoms—as of the strongest jasmine. All the while you and I were singing verse after verse of the hymn while processing around each flourishing tree of our orchard cemetery. Our steps were positively sprightly and forceful. I noted particularly how my own limbs felt more like lovely young tree limbs than arms and legs.

While we became energetic parts of the procession of dazzling color and smell that danced among us, we each saw with our inner senses at the same moment that our own lives by the grace of God had been fruitful: what it felt like to be fruitful trees that could green anew each year at Christ's resurrection. It was a deeply reverenced moment, and we sank to our knees in unison as I intoned a Te Deum.

The last part of the dream was strangest of all. We were now seated on small benches at that gravesite whose identity I had some six months ago obscured with my staff so none of my women would have trouble denying knowledge of its location to any investigating clerical authorities. You know all about this, I am sure, since little else has consumed my outward activities for so long. At any rate, at this point in the dream I admit to some human satisfaction in the knowledge that the soul of our young man at last rests in peace, and that we are here seated comfortably on his gravesite. Each of us has a writing table, and we are laboring at some manuscripts with texts and neumes. Suddenly, and with the utmost gentleness, you pick up the table that is in front of me at the same time that yours simply disappears. What was my table you place between us and becomes more an altar. We stand, arms raised. You say softly, as if chanting, that I must know that the writing I have just been working at is not really the essence of what transcribing or translating the Voice of Wisdom has been for me. I look in some perplexity as the familiar Voice fills my ears. Then my arms and hands move gracefully on their own, describing neume shapes and arcs that are living banners of human flesh, rosy and beautiful but shaped like some rippling bands of seaweed. They sound and float from my fingers toward the table between us. I see you smiling, light streaming all around you as the bands of flesh configure the body of Christ.

April 22, 1179
Third Sunday after Easter

Trying to imagine the shape and direction of our two houses when I am gone would be my last big distraction—a terrible waste of my now much-diminished energy. The familiarity of that latter phrase is of course an old distraction, one I have worried over for at least thirty years. Never have I been truly satisfied with the amount of physical energy at my command, even in my prime. Too often I have behaved like some tenant farmer's poor plow beast, harnessed to a specific task, the yoke a constraint rather than an instrument designed to perfect the adjustment of weight so the weight of a given task is distributed equitably. Stomping and straining, I push on until I am either victorious in the completion or so exhausted by the effort that illness enforces rest.

At my death, I leave small gatherings of work in disarray. Guibert chides gently but regularly that we have for so long failed to put all of the music in better order. What he means to say is that, although several years ago we sent a collection of our sacred songs to the monks in Villers, we are without a finished fair copy for ourselves. Since then, we have added a few more of our songs to the singing of the liturgy. Even among the music we sent, small changes have occurred over years of regular singing. The truth is that the final version of any antiphon or sequence remains in my head, heart, and hand, and nothing could be clearer these days than the fact of their mortality. These so very physical parts of me deteriorate daily, and I thank

God that they are the expendable parts. Such is not true of the music; it deserves more of our attention now.

We have scribes skilled in notation who have been trained sufficient to the task. It is simply a matter of directing one of them to compare any original music we sing at Office and Mass for a given feast with whatever we have made of its written transcription in the past. Any corrections or revisions will then be made, and the pieces recopied. I must only clarify the order once again. The Marian music will retain a prominent place, followed by the special sequences for honored saints. All of the Ursula songs will join the Holy Innocents, and I must be sure that the old working copy of the *Ordo virtutum* is perfected and included at the end. Nothing of this could go forward during the last half-year because of the interdict. Now that our throats are finally freed from the silencing grip of the devil, let the preservation of music have the priority it deserves!

I fear the effort required repeatedly to answer the worldly charges of the prelates of Mainz has robbed me of my last remaining physical strength, yet I hear myself nearly as an echo, I have said the same fear so many times before, and who am I to know? For months—ever since I began writing to our oppressors at Mainz the long letter about the salvific power of music—the suspicion has been with me that the energy fueling the work was no longer in any way physical. Which means it need not be finite.

Such glimpses into the greatest mysteries are nowhere so dramatic as the visions I have so long received. The brilliant reds and blues, the glittering gold and silver sheen are in abeyance, behind a different door. This particular sense of energy that if not finite is much more subtle, extremely fragile though immortal, is vulnerable to human doubts and predicaments. More like tapping into a sacred breathing. When falling into its rhythm, I feel the possibility for subsuming this frail form as a promise of unbelievable sweetness.

April 29, 1179
Fourth Sunday after Easter

This is simply what today brings, I tell myself. I yearn to accept simplicity along with the reprieve of our sound. Simplicity is not my gift. With what speed and how ungratefully I now begin to catalog what still remains to organize before death, as if I were the one to determine the completion of time, or that my own efforts could turn the tide of history. No sooner are we risen indeed with Christ and able to ground without fear the poor young man whose body nearly served as scapegoat for the restless ambitions of the absent Archbishop Christian and his minions—no sooner does divine Wisdom triumph over jealous pride—than I twitch with the responsibilities that remain. And why do they present themselves so importantly? Simply because I am still alive and able to push them around like muddy dregs in unclarified broth.

I still walk. Staff in one hand, a carved ash stick in the other, branched at the bottom with a stout trileg to disperse what tends more and more toward the ground. With one young woman sturdily under each bent elbow, I hardly need to touch the ground. Legs merely shuffle and paw the earth, the upper body nearly floats—a strange sensation that resembles walking only in the sense that it moves me from one place to the other. It reminds me of all those trips on the Rhine when I merely perched in the boat while someone paddled or poled. Some other forces redoubled the current of the river, or countered it, while my senses soaked in the ever changing light and its lively play on the water, or gathered a myriad of fresh data that sank nearly unbeknownst to me deep into my soul. There for years they might swim darkly, inchoate but with the blind assurance of tadpoles in the March brook, emerging only when touched by the finger of God into coherent patterns in the form of sung praise, watery dreams, or dazzling visions. For so long have I been navigated, with such skill and ease in a perennially ailing body!

Strange that this ancient body persists in the illusion that it must keep on moving, when all along, from so many decades past, it has been aided by women, men, machines, animals, the divine breath, and especially the will of God. It must be mind then, and not the body at all, that pushes like a flying insect cornered, buzzing as it gropes wildly, terrified it will be squashed out before finding an opening back to its real element, the wide sky.

Great Silence befriends, allows me to look and listen in the mornings if I can manage to still the buzzing in my mind. Whispering birds waken me, sounding the air like instruments playing—lisping flutes, trilling whistles, and nasal honks. Plum branches in the orchard burst into puffy sleeves of white clouds, long straight arms so heavily riddled with clumped blossoms it is a wonder they do not break from the weight. Their odor floats like smoke.

May 10, 1179
Ascension Thursday

She is so like music—her way of movement entirely in time and not space. For me, it is not possible to make music unless it moves in space as well as time, but for Hanna, blind from infancy, the pattern of the universe unrolls itself in time rather than space.

I'm trying to remember which of us discovered how exaggerated Hanna's sense of time was; it was not I. It must have been Clothild, blind herself, though only in adulthood—and that, very gradually—not nearly born blind, like Hanna. Clothild had learned to walk, move, and view the world's furnishings in their places and spacings—the distances between trees in a field, the depth of stairs, the way we all in a sense are framed each day in a landscape stretching outwardly to the horizon, then extended through our inner eyes and knowledge to the vault of heaven. Even that inner space has shape and volume for most of us, and Clothild always managed to retain a sense of such things. I suppose it came from a sharp memory of the years of her childhood, riding horses around planted fields, wading through streams in forests, viewing the vertical planes of mountainsides. Years after taking her vows with us, and slowly, Clothild's vision began to change. Each eye admitted a narrower and narrower circle for sight, and what they each saw could be joined into one picture only by virtue of all that accumulated experience held in memory. Occasionally she confessed that she yearned to refresh that experience.

When Hanna came to us as a young novice, it never

occurred to me at first that she had learned a world so different from the rest of us. My novice mistress reported that blindness was no impediment to Hanna's becoming literate, because her memory and ear for music were excellent. She had all one hundred fifty psalms and their cadences within the first months of her novitiate. Hymns and sequences, especially those that had rhyme and meter, or even an irregular but characteristic rhythm, she learned as quickly as any of my women gifted in music. Choral propers of the Mass were more difficult, and something of the liturgy was missing in her experience—I see now it must be that element we think of as spatial.

Even learning to read was not so difficult for Hanna. She quickly discovered how her keen sense of touch discerned the tracings of the pen along the vellum. The slight incising our eyes ignore was decipherable to her fingers. Even better for her were wax tablets with the stylus, whose incision was so much more clearly defined, and we had Karl construct a set of wax tablets especially for her use. We never set her to work regularly in the scriptorium, however, because she couldn't master scribal copying. She listened and wrote feverishly, but in her haste to check the shapes she had made, the ink smeared and letters blurred. Without that checking, she couldn't be sure exactly where her pen had just been, only how long a time it had been moving. I even tried having someone seated beside her sprinkling sand as she wrote, hoping in that way to make the drying process catch up with her involuntary rubbing and checking of what she had just written, but it never really succeeded. I would hear laughter and know that the sand was being swept every which way, and the result would be general confusion and merriment, which included herself, for Hanna's way was always to enter the enjoyment of any mayhem she created. Before the end of her novitiate, we knew that her talents would not make her useful in the scriptorium.

Much later, after she was professed, I would call specially for her when I was ill. Her care was balm. When she tended to feet, for example, or rubbed oil into joints of hands or arms, it was not so much having feet rubbed as having them discovered anew, digit after digit, working back to the heel and sequentially up to each part of the ankle joint.

Hanna was so sensitive to sound and rhythm that she identified each of us by the way we walked. Not that she didn't also explore our faces. Sometimes at a choir practice, and while still a young novice, she would walk among us, singing and listening as she combined a sister's voice with a particular chin, open mouth, cheekbones, eyes, and brow. But she knew us best, and even from a distance, by our characteristic gait.

More elemental things, like rain, fire, or frost, Hanna knew over great distances. Again, it was as if space or distance did not exist for her. We grew to rely on her for information about when to cover or pick crops against frost or when we could expect much-needed rain in the kitchen garden. I think she discerned such things with her nose. Her sense of smell was uncanny and sufficiently complex for me to trust her absolutely deciphering medicinal ingredients.

As she ages, Hanna's faculties for knowing remain keen, her singing strong. Her speaking voice used to trouble me greatly. Of all my women, she had the most difficulty learning to maintain the prescribed Great Silence. We would hear her speak out at any time—never in refectory, while eating—but at nearly any other time we might hear her exclaiming about the beauty of something or the difficulty of something at hand.

Ever since Godfrey first and then Guibert began questioning me about the history of my visions, I have thought much more about such things. It occurs to me now how many different ways of seeing exist. For years I supposed that my way of seeing with both inner and outer eyes was not so unusual, though there was always a reason I was afraid to tell anyone about the experiences with inner eyes. The fiery brilliance of the inner universe must surely have been frightening when first seen, though it is hard to remember that fear in any detail. The inner world has for so long been my preferred and longed-for familiar. Memory is yet another way to move and see in the world. For Clothild, for example, memories of colors and space and even felt landscapes allowed her to continue living nearly as a sighted person, but in turn limit her ability to change. Hanna learns everything she knows using hands, ears, and nose for eyes. Those, plus her inner eyes: for although she does not see what I see, she sees an inner world whose beauty and variety fill her with joy when she is so visited. Most difficult of all to imagine is the possibility that many people—some of them even under my care and direction—see only with their outer eyes, and devour greedily for their own personal satisfaction what of beauty they see.

May 20, 1179
Feast of Pentecost

This evening after Compline they helped me test my legs with a brief walk to the infirmary, our singing still in my head, the simple goodness of hearing the joined praise of our voices. I was reminded of Wilhelmina. She told me that when our blessed singing of the Office resumed, the music we made was not as full as what she had learned to listen for these past months during Lent while we were suffering without sung melodies. She was surprised, even disappointed, she confessed: she wondered whether we were simply out of practice after many months and so the music we produced compared unfavorably with the memory she holds of how we had once sounded.

What a mysterious process in which we participate when we make music! So much listening is required in order to breathe out inspired sound. I doubt that Wilhelmina carries in her head a frozen memory of some specific Lauds or Vespers we sang this past Advent. She has grown into a fine cantrix, and the music within her is always growing and changing, I am sure. Rather than a fixed memory of something completed in the past, music is more likely a thing that changes all the time. The tempi and degrees of loudness vary, individual voices stand out from time to time, decorate the movement of the melody ever so slightly like the curling tendril of a growing vine. What she hears may change according to the way the birds sang in their roost at dawn that day, or with the distant song of a vinedresser at work.

Years ago I spoke to a sculptor about a similar process, when I was on tour. In a monastery at Trier I was struck by a statue of Our Lady emerging out of a fruitwood log like a butterfly from its chrysalis. But much slower, and the abbot complained at the length of time it was taking for the work to be completed. For weeks the woodcarver had not even touched his tools, said the abbot, and each time the abbot came hopefully to inspect the progress, there was nothing to see except the sculptor in puzzled contemplation.

This was not laziness or delay, I knew, for the woman emerging from the log now had a bended knee that propelled her forward into motion, lips parted in praise, amazed and open eyes, with a head tilted slightly back and up in ecstatic listening. She nearly breathed, and I spoke at length with the man who limned her. His name was Simon, and as answer to the abbot's impatient complaint, Simon explained to me that for weeks on end his all-consuming daily task was simply to look. He considered various logs with variations in shape and color. He walked in complete circles around them, changing the angle of his gaze. He sat at their bases, towered over them looking down, looked from a distance and up very close. He studied the figure of a holy woman illuminated in a copy they had of the Book of the Apocalypse, of the woman clothed in the sun. He took in the colors and lines, the expression on her face, the feel of her feet supported by the moon. In his mind's eye, he combined both the log he had by then chosen and the painted image, then fed both of those with the glorious text it proclaimed. He called to mind particular sunsets, summer and winter night skies, in order to observe possible colors and shadows. All of these and more formed a wonderfully liquid chaotic mixture that bubbled in a mass like March tadpoles in their jelly, whirling an undifferentiated dance for days as his saturated eyes grew dizzy with love. Only after the form itself was clearly limned inside his own body could he dare move his hand to coax its transfer, trusting that what now lived inside him might emerge as well in the log transformed.

This was his required listening, lengthy, exhausting, bone-crushing in its demands on faith. Such I think has been the silence imposed on Wilhelmina, and I wonder how its blossom will sound.

June 5, 1179
Feast of St. Boniface, Bishop and Martyr

Guibert's learned visitor leaves today on pilgrimage. He intends going to Canterbury cathedral, where Britain's loyal archbishop was so brutally cut down. People flock to honor the sainted Thomas at the shrine that marks the place of martyrdom; even his king arrived there to do public penance after too many years of living with his own culpability.

I am far too old to be chosen for the crown of martyrdom, I noted wryly to the two men as we talked after chapter yesterday, and it is such a rarity in our own times. Yet the fact of martyrdom, its power for all who are pulled into its wake, is there for our reflection, a great part of our history as monastics. Martyrdom literally encourages us—gives us the courage to push forward and rethink the meanings of concepts like apostasy and *contemptus mundi*[29] in terms of a world that has so little regard for virtue.

For holy instruction all people of faith look to the saints—especially those who are martyrs—as exemplars of the holy life lived to its fullest. And perpetually wonder at the face of martyrdom—the requisite bravery, the difficult choices, the loneliness it entails. But in a deeper way none of that is the issue, for true martyrdom chooses us. More to the point, and what is especially clear in the case of Becket, is how we religious deal with the world and the rules the world fabricates to increase and perpetuate its power and influence over us. How does the good shepherd tend his flock in such a power-hungry world? That was Becket's dilemma, as it has so recently been mine.

The more the institutions of secular kingdoms proliferate and the more they centralize, the more they tend to usurp prerogatives originally designated to serve the sacred. Adding pointedly to this cancerous increase is an archbishop such as ours in Mainz, who is never *in* Mainz, but rather exercises his complex intelligence in the secular world as chancellor to the emperor Barbarossa. He has quite simply abandoned his flock, left them to marauding wolves and sycophantic prelates. And yet it is by authority of the errant shepherd that our interdict is finally lifted.

Mother of God, how it all dissolves thankfully in the incense of roses! Our garden just now thrums with sounds, drips with colors. Roses climb the rock walls, exuding perfume of deepest pink and rich cream. Overnight, purple spires of delphinium seem to tower over clumps of poppies, whose blossoms are the most delicately tissued shades of peach, pink, and salmon. Inebriate bees, householding birds—nature explodes in its courting ritual for the sake of Jerusalem. Outside whose walls the world lays claim, conquers, sacrifices beauty over and over again.

June 24, 1179, Solstice
Fifth Sunday after Pentecost

Finally, now, I begin to trust what I have for years schooled myself to believe: that the care and management at Mount St. Rupert and Eibingen after my death cannot be my concern. Both my houses are in order. Mass and Office are sung with regularity and according to the Rule. The usual discord that bubbles underneath seems minimal, whether because of my growing detachment from daily details or the euphoric, celebratory air that rushed in with the lifting of the interdict. Perhaps a little of both. It makes easier relinquishing the office I have carried for so many decades.

Already I sense my absence in subtle ways, as in the singing. I hear psalms sung faster, rhythms not quite the same in the antiphons. Even those pieces that had their first hearing through me are changed—new in some ways to my ears, even though they are now notated and recorded for future generations as I first heard them. It has been more than a year since I have directed them with arm and hand, considerably longer since my singing voice commanded their following. Cantrices of both houses and novice mistress here have long been the real teachers, and the sounds that issue are quite different to my ears.

I remember years ago when Basel first told me that some aspects of our singing reflected my own physiognomy—the way I moved and walked, even my breathing and temperament to some extent. I was indignant and even angered by his suggestion, which seemed to contradict constant efforts to serve as clear vessel to whatever came through me. At the time I felt that my capacity to receive visions, come forth with new music, and maintain the gift of prophecy with integrity was entirely dependent on scraping away at personal ambitions, with no care for how the world might respond. In proof of fact, I reminded my dear friend heatedly, it was precisely my fear of criticism by men—influential and recognized authorities in the Church—that for so long made it impossible for anything to come through me. It came only after so many years of suffering, as if I had to burn away concerns for the opinions of others—as if the searing pains were layers of skin that needed peeling away—and here came Basel positing that the shapes and sounds of the music I taught the women had something to do with my own deep configuration!

He was not altogether incorrect, though it is only within the last year that I understand what he meant.

When the cantrix stands before my sisters, they follow not only her motions; they tend to breathe where she breathes, marking phrases where she marks them. Something more: I sense her state of mind is reflected back in the music we hear—her intentions, any personal worries, her movement through the whole of the piece, her regard for its very form. These subtleties in turn affect the same considerations in the members of the choir. Once in a while it happens that the cantrix is poised directly in relation to the mystery itself; then the singers, thinking each and all that they are simply following her, allow themselves to be led to the mystery undistracted. Here is music of heavenly contemplation. Even so, and for all the fortuitous interlacing of grace and hard labor, Basel was not wrong in what he said to me. Our nature is not that of angels. We are humanly wrapped, souls clothed intimately in our bodies for life.

July 22, 1179
Feast of St. Mary Magdalene

My women rarely approach to ask for my time anymore. I think the turning point came with the battle over the interdict. They could see how consuming it was to grapple with so many players—identify who was friend and who foe—how lonely to map and revise complex strategies without Volmar's receptive ear, and how withering to the health of us all the practise of prayer with no music. At any rate, they have observed my less-than-dependable health for years, noted that I have even outlived a lifelong secretary, and I see in their eyes I am ancient. Guibert is exuberant in restraining visitors who wish to consult me from the outside. In this he is both protective and demanding, since his concern is ferreting choice prophetic biographical particulars. He perhaps dreams of canonization for me; I meanwhile cherish the solitude.

What a surprise when Christina passed a note at Compline requesting a meeting: In consideration of Great Silence, I make this request in writing. —It was, I hoped, of godly matters we would speak.

In consideration of the heat, I met her in the cloister, where this summer Karl has fashioned a chair for me that is gentle on sharp bones. It receives me with such comfort because that clever man has woven both the back and the seat with strong prunings from the vineyard, covered simply with a length of flaxen cloth. It is the way the fiery, brilliant orioles nest themselves in the peach tree, I told him, or like the finest cradle for rocking a firstborn son.

Christina approached, did obeisance, then lifted her full face like a sunflower, snappy brown eyes so dark they are nearly black. Not even a single drop of moisture around her mouth or forehead in this weather, while I feel familiar little rivulets of sweat running on my own skin under the draperies. I touch the smoothness of her cheek with pleasure, always wondering where it is that this woman of such violent extremes finally harnesses and buries her periods of torture. She rises to sit on the stone bench that lines the north wall, and only in that movement do I see any evidence of her age—that she has already spent over a quarter of a century with us and that she was past adolescence when she entered. Her knees are getting old, one in particular that slips out of proper connection with one of the bones of her lower leg. I have treated her more often in recent years, but only her knees.

She tells me she has been thinking about my *Scivias* visions, the ones Volmar and I were still working on when she came to join us at Disibodenberg. She talks of a few in particular, of her concern for those people who want to know of them and cannot read, of what will happen to them after my death. When I show some impatience with her uncharacteristic meandering, she suddenly pulls from her sleeve a small piece of parchment, which she unrolls to show me in such a way that the setting sun catches it aslant, and its dazzling beauty makes me groan aloud.

Later

Something was amiss. Not so at first glance, which took my breath away, but within seconds, and increasingly. One of the obvious things about Christina's painting is that it had nothing to do with any of the *Scivias* visions. What had inspired the miniature was the Sequence for St.

Ursula—specifically its climax, portrayed in fire and blood juxtaposed with the serpent being suffocated by a choker of pearls exquisitely subtle in range of color and shading.[30] But that wasn't what was disturbing. Ursula was being consumed by fire so alive it danced on the page. A river of blood streamed. It was as though the painter herself were pinned in each detail to such an extent that any transforming music was cut off. The longer I gazed, the more it seemed as though some dark vision had begun to emerge through Christina which she then stifled by turning to literal details of the slaughter of Ursula. The human painter had seized control of brushes, colors, and shapes sufficient to block any possibility of allowing the divine Voice continuance. Faith and freedom had no dominion.

As I might have expected, Christina at first tried not to understand what had gone awry, preferring to hear what I told her as criticism of her artistic abilities or a way in which she was mistaken in her interpretation of what she thought of as *my* vision of St. Ursula. Finally, I took her hands in mine, had her close her eyes and open her heart and thoughts to what might move beyond the confines of the two of us.

Gradually I felt her still, collect, stir and begin to allow passage. I asked her then gently to leave her eyes closed and move in a small space in the cloister, simply focusing on the evening call of a nearby mockingbird and feeling my close presence in order to know she would not move so far to one side as to bump into the wall or stumble against some physical obstruction. I did not ask her to tell me what she might be seeing with her inner senses that moved through her body, but her dancing was inspired, the fluid drapery of her clothing adding to its beauty as if from within.

Long periods of Christina's dance were horizontal

and close to the floor, like the movement of some ancient river at its mouth, not as it arises fresh in a mountain source, but as it reaches a dark confluence, issues at last into a larger body like the salt sea. As the dancing more and more filled the space of the cloister, it was like seeing fire move through a field at the end of the season, igniting dried vegetation in bright color as it consumed and heated the air around it. Her concentration included mine and extended so long that we were blanketed in soft darkness at the end, though it was still easy to discern movement since the darkness had come on so very gradually.

When she had finished there was long silence and meeting of the eyes between us. Finally she got up to leave and winced as the bad knee buckled. She moved away, slowly and limping, to her cell. The most remarkable thing about Christina's long dance was that in all its dark beauty I detected nothing of fear.

August 15, 1179
Feast of the Assumption of the Virgin

Their hands like soft-whispering lips prepare my body for journey. Young fingers on my old toes, smoothing with oil the sharp calluses of gnarled feet with skin like horn. Drops of fresh water and weakened white wine gently flush withered lips so last sounds of praise are still possible, can swim in air like golden fish.

> Alleluia, alleluia. I am highest fiery power that kindled all living sparks: and no mortal thing have I dismissed without understanding it, flying in spires with wings loft of wisdom and ordering all things well. And I am fiery life of that Name which burnishes the beauty of fields and scintillates the waters; that burns in sun, moon, and stars; and, with my flowing breath of invisible life, I arouse all things to live and I sustain the entirety. That breath lives in greenness and flowering, and the waters flow as if alive: even the sun lives in the glow of that breath, such that if moon should fail, sun would enkindle it and it would live anew; and the stars, they too live in my breath.
>
> I established columns that support the whole orb of earth. And I established those winds of lesser wings that in their calm sustain the stronger breath, lest the stronger, unbounded, might fly dangerously off. In just that way does the body shelter and support the soul, lest it perish. And even as the stronger winds animate their lesser ones so they might harmoniously exercise their offices, so my breath in the soul holds the body together, so it does not fail.

> Wherefore I am also that fiery force lying hidden in things ardent inside from me, the way the flame always moves within the fire, the way the breath continually sets body to motion. All these are deeply alive, nor is death found in them, for I am life. For I am the reckoning, breath of the sounding Word through whom all things were made, and there can be no generation of death in what I have breathed, who am life. I am life inextinguishable, not sparked by stones or budded from branches, not rooted in the strong seed of man: rather, all that lives is rooted in me. This reckoning is the root, and it flowers by sounding the Word in truth.[31]

Flames above the candles held in their hands still quiver, telling them the breath still moves in me. Motes of shimmering light-soaked dust rain down from the casement. My tired eyes devour them one by one and altogether. How can eyes so worn be yet so eager, so hungry for still more light? *I am resurrection and life,* they seemed to sing, as if beginning the Communion of my Requiem; but no, still *I am highest fiery power.* More life, more breath. Light in the body, movement.

Later

Will they then feel orphaned when it finally does happen, though they have all been instructed for their lives about the joy of this passage? About the beauty of the cycles we observe? Unless the seed falls daily, we have been instructed. All who live mothered by liturgy are pulled directly into the inexorable movement of the year, greenness into the ripening of seed. Only twice in this long life did I seem to fall out of that rhythm. Hundreds of deaths witnessed, attended, celebrated, only two threatened to orphan me, and one of the two I did not witness. Rikkarda's death now over a score of years behind, she snatched so young and far from her nest with us. Yet it was not her death but her flight from us that orphaned. In time I could understand that in her untimely death she was reunited with us. We sang her back, celebrated her bodily death in Mass and Office, immortalized her spirit in the *Ordo virtutum,* and left self-pitying grief behind.

The orphaned loneliness came again, unexpectedly and painfully, with Volmar's death. His was timely in old age; he was ripe for the passage after the decades of loving service, generous instruction that molded his life, but a devastating loss nevertheless in a way I had not experienced before, nor have again. It was at the time of the final shaping of the last book of visions, *De operatione dei.* Briefly then even the liturgy was at a remove from me. The gathering of that last book of visions had taken a decade. Preaching tours intervened, letters, construction of the daughter house, Lord, how many lengthy bouts of illness! Catching the visions with discernment was difficult, finding their order even harder, and Volmar was indispensable. Through all the interventions he held my place, and when he died it was lost for a time. Something about those late visions was too fiery, much more akin to ecstasy than those from earlier times, and I knew that in receiving and giving form to several I was pulled dangerously out of balance, into fire that could consume me. So much had I come to rely on his gentle weight on my course, so long had I known it as ballast rather than most valuable offering of inestimable service, that his death—though peaceful in itself—sent me into a pit of searing loss. Against all reason, in spite of all belief.

Over time, like a poor weasel slithering in water, I

learned to swim under the darkness, found my way back to the liturgy through the faint shadow that moved, watery, before me. Searing light was absent, though not the beauty. Eventually I was a creature of liturgical life again, renewed and darkened, able to live much more in that world of beauty than in the world of everyday duties and satisfactions. Never again—even through the seemingly endless morass of our lives under the interdict—was there any doubt which was the greater reality, and visits with Volmar, some in dream, others waking, became frequent and looked for.

August 28, 1179
Feast of St. Augustine, Bishop and Doctor

They are burning the fields today; the powerfully acrid, eye-smarting smell drifts on the air like late summer incense. Many families of swallows that have darted back and forth over our cloister, tirelessly and without noise since late spring, gather now in noisy chapter each evening after Vespers. Perched on the crowns of our fullest maples, they sing the sun down in full community. When we return from Compline they are gone, I know not where, but next evening they gather noisily once more. It seems they wait for a signal invisible to my eyes. Not temperature, for some years they disappear in an untimely spell of heat, and others on a day of fresh, seasonal breezes. Still, they wait for something. Through all their flutter and chatter, they are attentive. I have long admired their luster and sleek shapes, how perfectly they move in their element—their forked tails and wedge-shaped wings fitting them into perfect machinery for flying. Now I see that they attend to something more subtle. I also wait.

September 8, 1179
Feast of the Nativity of the Virgin

End-of-summer thrumming is constant, yet so soft and underneath it is hard to listen for. They bring me bouquets of burnished marigolds and ragged asters. Darkness comes earlier every day.

When they look at me with sad questioning eyes, what they are really wondering is how and when I can let go of the world.

Now finally we speak openly of my death. Some of them weep, become like lost children, question me. Where will I be? What will be for them? I instruct them in presence. What presence is. I ask whether I am now present to them, and they all feel it strongly. Then I point out how little activity I have achieved lately, how infrequently at refectory, absent for weeks from choir practice. Two new novices would not recognize my face, but know my presence.

I remind them of their own novitiates. How unfamiliar and forbidding the way of life seemed at first. What bitter lessons are required to make an offering of oneself—to be an oblate—when one often doesn't yet have any awareness of what there is to offer. How many constant reminders many of them required. How firmly their novice mistress needed to mirror this one's habitual petulance, another's perpetual seeking after attention by coughing in choir, drawing everyone's gaze with nervous tics and ejaculated phrases, witty observations.

I further remind them of particular instances of presence we have experienced together; then singly, as they have confessed privately to me. Everyone recalls the times on Ursula's feast day, when we felt her move among us, when her being saturated our every step in procession and her cries rang in our ears. You must further remember and meditate on what St. Paul told us about dying in his first letter to the Corinthians.

> Someone may ask, "How are dead people raised, and what sort of body do they have when they come back?" They are stupid questions. Whatever you sow in the ground has to die before it is given new life, and the thing that you sow is not what is going to come; you sow a bare grain, say of wheat or something like that, and then God gives it the sort of body that He has chosen: each sort of seed gets its own sort of body. Everything that is flesh is not the same flesh: there is human flesh, animals' flesh, the flesh of birds, and the flesh of fish. Then there are heavenly bodies and there are earthly bodies; but the heavenly bodies have a beauty of their own and the earthly bodies a different one. The sun has its brightness, the moon a different brightness, and the stars a different brightness. It is the same with the resurrection of the dead: the thing that is sown is perishable, but what is raised is imperishable.[32]

It is like preparing for a big feast, I tell them. Think of Christmas or Epiphany, even Pentecost. Music must be learned, lessons studied, a certain amount of penance, mild fasting, assiduous reflection about the meaning of texts. Meanwhile, the presence shimmers like a gold thread through it all.

I remind them about the women who observed with their own eyes the continuum of Christ's death and resurrection, who were so prepared in love as to recognize his presence among them, and still he was changed beyond all recognition, except in his presence.

Ego sum resurrectio et vita, "I am resurrection and life: who believes in me, even though he die, will live; and all who live in me will not die for ever." We sing and have sung together how many times that Communion of the Requiem? How could he have dared to say that if it were anything but true? As for myself, I look forward to being more of the substance of the stars. I long to be numbered with poets of divinity, inscribed in the line of ageless Wisdom receptacles, bearers of particles of light in the universe. I desire to be like Strabo of the ninth century—equally at home in the sensuous beauties of a monastic garden while in this earthly body and as conjoined in the universe's praise thereafter.

[*Let these adore thee, ever-almighty,*
and tell their blessings throughout the ages!
  Stars on their axes dancing in chorus,
  and sun, their sister, light of the heavens:
Let these adore thee, ever-almighty . . .
  Thus too, the meteors falling through heaven
  and dew from rains that nourish the spirit:
Let these adore thee, ever-almighty . . .
  So fire and seething with bone-drying heat,
  the frigid burning and frost in gardens:
Let these adore thee, ever-almighty . . .
  Snowfall and ice rain, nightfall and daylight,
  flashes of lightning outlining cloudbanks:
Let these adore thee, ever-almighty . . .
  The arid mountains that spring forth new hills
  and founts of waters, their streams resounding:
Let these adore thee, ever-almighty,
and tell their blessings throughout the ages!][33]

Notes

Part One

Translations from the Latin, unless otherwise specified, are the author's. For specifics about the parts of the Mass and Divine Office, see the glossary.

1. The opening of the Exultet, chanted by the deacon during the Paschal Vigil.

2. Accounts of the extended papal schism of which Hildegard speaks and the terms of the Peace of Venice signed July 24, 1177, are clarified in Alfred Haverkamp, *Medieval Germany 1056–1273* (New York: Oxford Univ. Press, 1988).

3. For the Latin text of Hildegard's letter, see J. B. Pitra, *Sanctae Hildegardis Opera* (Monte Cassino, 1882), Epistle 37, pp. 523–24.

4. For texts and discussion of Hildegard's letters to Barbarossa, see Marianna Schrader and A. Adelgundis Führkötter, *Die Echtheit de Schrifttums der heiligen Hildegard von Bingen* (Köln-Graz, 1956), pp. 124–31.

5. Hildegard's last book of visions, very much concerned with describing the universe in terms of microcosm and macrocosm, was written between 1163 and 1174. A Latin text is in *Patrologia Latina* (hereinafter *PL*), vol. 197, ed. J. P. Migne (Paris: Palmé, 1855), and an English translation has been published as *Hildegard of Bingen's Book of Divine Works,* ed. Matthew Fox (Santa Fe: Bear and Co., 1987).

6. Guibert of Gembloux, long an admirer of Hildegard's work, served as her last secretary and scribe, from 1177 until her death in 1179. For the Latin text of Hildegard's letter, see Pitra, *Sanctae Hildegardis Opera,* pp. 407–15.

7. Pope Alexander's letter to Wezelin was written in 1173, responding to Hildegard's pleading for his help: "Alexander, servant of the servants of God, to our beloved son, abbot of St. Andrew in Cologne, greetings and apostolic blessings. On behalf of our beloved daughter in Christ, Hildegard, prioress of Mount St. Rupert in Bingen and of the sisters of that place, you should know that it has come to our attention that when, according to their custom, they had elected for themselves a master and provost from the monastery of St. Disibod, the abbot of that place was unwilling to acknowledge the election of the person from his monastery, and even up to the present time still refuses to assign that person to them. Wherefore since it is proper that there be provision for the aforementioned sisters in those things which pertain to the salvation of their souls, we mandate to your discretion through apostolic writings that you call together both sides to your presence once you have made inquiry into this and have more clearly understood this matter of the election of the

provost. Then decide the case with proper justice. And if these sisters cannot have a provost from that monastery, see to it, at least, that they have a competent one from another." (Joseph L. Baird and Rodd K. Ehrman, trans., *The Letters of Hildegard of Bingen,* vol. 1 [New York: Oxford Univ. Press, 1994], letter 10r, pp. 46–47).

8. Godfrey's brief term as secretary ended with his death in 1176. The *Vita* begun by Godfrey was completed by a monk named Theodoric after Hildegard died. See the Latin text of the *Vita* in *PL,* vol. 197, and a good English translation by Anna Silvas in four successive volumes of the Australian Benedictine periodical *Tjurunga,* vols. 29–32.

9. The Latin texts for these commentaries are in *PL,* vol. 197. For an English translation of her commentary on the Rule, see Hugo Feiss, "Hildegard von Bingen: Explanation of the Rule of St. Benedict," in *Vox benedictina* 7:2.

10. *Benedicere digneris, Domine, hoc scriptorium famulorum tuorum, ut quidquid scriptum fuerit, sensu capiant, opere perficiant. See* George H. Putnam, *Books and Their Makers During the Middle Ages,* vol. 1 (Hillary House, 1962), p. 61. Trans. R. John Blackley.

11. Ludwig became abbot of St. Eucharius in 1168. Hildegard wrote the music and text of a sequence honoring St. Maximin for Abbot Ludwig.

12. Hildegard's sung morality play *Ordo virtutum* was completed and performed between 1151 and 1152. A critical edition of the Latin text is available in Peter Dronke's *Poetic Individuality in the Middle Ages* (New York: Oxford Univ. Press, 1970), chap. 5. Dronke's excellent English translation of the play, with the Latin on facing pages, is to be found in his book *Nine Medieval Latin Plays* (Cambridge Univ. Press, 1994).

Part Two

13. See n. 5. Hildegard speaks here of a change in her vision of the order and shape of the cosmos, exemplified visually for us by comparing an illumination of her Cosmic Egg, "Das Weltall" (Tafel 4, Schau I 3 in *Hildegard von Bingen Wisse Die Wege* [Salzburg: Otto Müller, 1954]), with the illumination "Der Kosmosmensch" (facing p. 49 in *Hildegard von Bingen Welt und Mensch* [Salzburg: Otto Müller, 1965]).

14. Cf. St. Irenaeus, *The Demonstration of the Apostolic Preaching,* trans. J. Armitage Robinson (London: SPCK, 1920), p. 100.

15. The exact dates for these events: Becket murdered, December 29, 1170; Becket canonized, February 21, 1173; King Henry II does public penance, July 12, 1174.

16. *In rama sonat gemitus,* in Wolfenbüttel, Herzog-august-Bibliothek, MS 628, f. 168, earliest surviving piece of music about Becket. Probably from 1164 to 1170, since it mentions his exile in France. In the text, Rama = Canterbury; Rachel = Mater Ecclesia; son of Herod = Henry II; Joseph, sold by his jealous brothers = Becket.

17. *Vox in Rama audita est, ploratus, et ululatus: Rachel plorans filios suos, et noluit consolari; quia non sunt.* Matt. 2:18, quoting Jer. 31:15; also used in Gospel for the Feast.

18. Old Testament Lesson of Mass honoring Martyrs, Wis. 3:1–8 (Knox translation).

19. Hildegard refers to her two medico-physical texts, known in Latin as *Physica* and *Causae et curae,* both written down between 1151 and 1158. A Latin text of the first is in *PL,* vol. 197; of the second, an edition edited by Paul Kaiser was published under its Latin name in Leipzig in 1903. Neither work has so far a complete translation in English, though many sections are excerpted in various works written about Hildegard's knowledge and practice of medicine.

20. The complete Latin text, as Hildegard's "Epistola XLVII," is in *PL,* vol. 197, pp. 218–43. A corrected Latin text for portions of the letter is in Peter Dronke, *Women Writers of the Middle Ages* (New York: Cambridge Univ. Press, 1984), pp. 314–15. This translation of a portion of the letter is by Lachman and Blackley.

21. Wis. 11:24–25, 27; Introit for the Mass on Ash Wednesday.

22. Ps. 1:2–3.

23. Antiphon sung at the Blessing of the Ashes.

24. Letter #10, Baird and Ehrman, *Letters of Hildegard,* pp. 45–46.

25. Hildegard's last extant letter (Latin text in *PL,* vol. 197), in which she quotes from Dan. 13:23.

26. Tract of three verses (XV) following Lesson IV in the Paschal Vigil (Exod. 15:1–3).

Part Three

27. If any doubt remains about the nature of the power behind this interdict, we have only to turn to the reply Hildegard ultimately received to her last letter to Archbishop Christian. The archbishop of Mainz follows the customary epistolary formulas appropriate to the times and the respective stations of the two correspondents, then informs Hildegard that he has written to his prelates at Mainz granting her the privilege of singing the Divine Offices again "on the condition that proof the dead man's absolution has been established by the testimony of reliable men." Christian closes his letter with the expected clement voice of sympathy for the suffering of the women that Hildegard had described to him, but not until he has reminded the abbess that "the Church held that the man buried in your churchyard had incurred the sentence of excommunication while he was alive, and although some doubt remained concerning his absolution, the fact that you disregarded the outcry of the clergy and acted as if this would cause no scandal in the Church was a very dangerous act, since the statutes of the holy fathers are inviolable. You should have waited for definitive proof based on the suitable testimony of good men in the presence of the Church." Baird and Ehrman, *Letters of Hildegard,* p. 83.

28. The text of the hymn is attributed to St. Ambrose (fourth century) and is used liturgically for Lauds from Low Sunday to the Ascension; translated by Blackley.

29. *Contemptus mundi,* scorn for the world, is one of the personified female virtues in Hildegard's morality play *Ordo virtutum*. Christ said to his disciples, "I pray not for the world" (John 17:9), perfectly voicing his defiance of the worldly values with which Hildegard has so recently done battle.

30. Hildegard's sequence for the Mass honoring the martyrdom of St. Ursula and the 11,000 Virgins ends with these words:

    Then everyone came to recognize
    How defiance of the world is like the mountain of Bethel.
    They even identified that sweetest fragrance of incense and myrrh,
    Because defiance of the world surpasses all perfumes.
    Then the devil fell into his own members
    Who slaughtered in those graceful bodies
    The noblest way of life.
    And all the elements heard this wrenching cry
    And themselves cried out before the throne of God:
    "Ach! the crimson blood of the innocent Lamb
    Is poured out in abundance with her marriage pledge." Let all the heavens hear this
    And with consummate music let them praise the Lamb of God,
    Because the throat of the ancient Serpent
    Is strangled in those pearls
    Who express in matter the Word of God.

31. This text, beginning with the words *Ego sum ignea vis,* is spoken by the divine image of a human being who appears at the opening of Part I, Vision 1 of *De operatione dei*. For the Latin text, see *PL,* vol. 197, pp. 743–44.

32. I Cor. 15:35–42.

33. *Omnipotentem semper adorent,* responsorial hymn composed by Walafrid Strabo, second quarter of the ninth century; in bifolio flyleaf to Laon, Bibliothèque Municipale, MS 266, translated by Blackley.

Glossary

NOTE: The characters of Basel, Christina, Wilhelmina, Hanna, and Clothild are fictional, developed to clarify the complex teachings and creative life of Hildegard; they are not listed here. For the terms Advent, Christmas, Epiphany, Lent, Easter, and Pentecost, see LITURGICAL SEASONS.

AARON'S ROD. According to Hebraic tradition, Moses' brother Aaron was confirmed in his priesthood by a miraculous sign: his staff burst into bloom and fruited with almonds (told in Num. 17:1–8).

AGNES, ST. Virgin-martyr venerated in Rome from the fourth century; liturgical texts for her feast became prototypes for liturgies of many other women saints. Since she was but a girl when she was tortured and martyred rather than deny the faith, and her name is a variant of the Latin *agnus* (lamb), she is frequently pictured holding a lamb, thus linking her to Christ, the Agnus Dei.

ALCUIN (CA. 735–804). Advisor to Charlemagne from 781; educator, poet, theologian, founder of two libraries, and abbot of Tours from 796. He was the chief inspiration of the Carolingian Renaissance.

ALEXANDER III, POPE (ca. 1100–1181). The first great lawyer-pope, from 1159 till his death; survived a schism of eighteen years, mostly in exile. Clashes with FREDERICK BARBAROSSA had begun as early as 1157; negotiations to end the schism began with the Peace of Venice in 1177. He presided over the Third Lateran Council in 1179, which established the lasting requirement that a two-thirds majority of cardinals be present at papal elections.

ALL SOULS. Commemoration of all the faithful departed by a MASS and OFFICE celebrated each November 2. The practice began with the BENEDICTINES in 998 and spread to Rome during the fourteenth century.

ANTIPHON. Brief text from PSALMS or Gospels sung before and after psalm verses in MASS and OFFICE, linking the psalm to the day's feast.

ASSUMPTION OF THE VIRGIN August 15 feast celebrating the belief that

Mary after death was assumed body and soul into heaven. Teaching first formulated in the West during the sixth century; in the East called the Dormition of Mary and observed as early as the fourth century.

ATHANASIAN CREED. Lengthy statement of beliefs erroneously ascribed to St. Athanasius, probably dating from the fifth century. It is concerned mainly with the Trinity and the Incarnation and carefully insists that belief in its tenets is necessary to salvation.

BARBAROSSA, see FREDERICK BARBAROSSA.

BASSUM. In the diocese of Bremen, north Germany, site of the monastery to which Hildegard's nun Rikkarda was called to serve as abbess.

BECKET, ARCHBISHOP THOMAS (CA. 1118–1170). Educated in law at Bologna and Auxerre; ordained deacon, then archdeacon at Canterbury in 1154. HENRY II appointed him chancellor in 1155. In 1162 he was elected archbishop of Canterbury; difficulties began with his friend Henry, and Becket soon resigned the chancellorship to dedicate his life to the church.

BEDE, VENERABLE (CA. 673–735). Benedictine monk at Jarrow. Great biblical scholar and one of the first historians of England.

BENEDICAMUS DOMINO. DEO GRATIAS. At the conclusion of the OFFICE hours: "Let us bless the Lord. Thanks be to God."

BENEDICTINES. Name given to communities of monks and nuns who live according to the RULE OF ST. BENEDICT; prevalent form of monasticism during the Middle Ages.

BERNARD OF CLAIRVAUX, ST. (1090–1153). Abbot of the Cistercian monastery of Clairvaux. It was Bernard who brought Hildegard's first visionary writing to the attention of the Cistercian pope Eugenius III, thence to approval by the Synod of Trier in the winter of 1147–48. Hildegard's letter to Bernard is extant.

BONIFACE, ST. (680–754). Britain-born, he converted great numbers of people in Germany after felling the sacred Oak of Thor at Geismar. Served briefly as the archbishop of Mainz; credited with significant reform of the Frankish Church. Martyred in Frisia; known as the "Apostle of Germany."

CALENDAR. Formal listing by month and date of the feasts of the TEMPORAL and SANCTORAL cycles.

CALLISTUS III, ANTIPOPE (D. CA. 1183). Claimant to the papacy from September 1168 to August 1178. Acknowledged as a pretender by the Peace of Venice, July 1177.

CANDLEMAS, see PURIFICATION.

CANTRIX. The woman soloist who intones a piece of chant, setting its pitch and mode, and sings major solo portions within the SCHOLA CANTORUM; frequently also the schola's director. The masculine form *cantor* may be used as a verb.

CARITAS. Love, the greatest of the theological virtues; its opposite, hatred, can take the form of indifference.

CATHARS. Name given to various heretical gnostic sects in Germany during the twelfth century; active in Cologne at the time of Hildegard's preaching ministries. Stamped out by orthodox Church. Similar beliefs were held by the Albigensians in southern France from the eleventh to the thirteenth century.

CATHEDRA. From the Latin; the bishop's chair or throne in his own cathedral church.

CHAPTER OF FAULTS. Religious exercise in which community members regularly advise one another of infractions committed against monastic RULE; held in the chapter house, so named because chapters from the Rule were read at daily meetings therein.

CHRISTIAN OF BUCH. Archbishop of Hildegard's diocese of Mainz from 1165 to 1183, though from 1171 on he was continually in imperial Italy, strategizing for FREDERICK BARBAROSSA. His predecessor, a supporter of ALEXANDER III, had been deposed by Frederick.

CISTERCIANS. Religious order founded in 1098 at Cîteaux to be a strict and pure reform of the BENEDICTINES. Its most famous member was BERNARD OF CLAIRVAUX. By the end of the twelfth century they had 530 abbeys in western Europe. They were noted for sheep and wool trade in England, for wine on the Continent.

DISIBODENBERG. Benedictine male monastery dedicated to St. Disibode; Hildegard lived there from 1106 to ca. 1151. The monastery, which was founded in the eighth century by Irish monks, was completely destroyed in the eighteenth century; archaeological excavation begun about 1986 is now nearly complete.

DIVINE OFFICE, see OFFICE.

DOMINA. Latin for "lady." *Domina* and *abbatissa* (abbess) were nearly interchangeable in the Middle Ages; Hildegard was addressed variously with one title or the other, also as *mater* (mother) and MAGISTRA.

EIBINGEN. Site of the daughter house Hildegard established in 1165 as an offshoot of RUPERTSBERG, directly across the Rhine. Suppressed in 1802 and eventually ruined. Known now as Rüdesheim-Eibingen, a new monastery was built there in 1900–4, called St. Hildegard's Abbey, as continuation of the monasteries at both Rupertsberg and Eibingen.

ELISABETH OF SCHÖNAU (1129–1165). German Benedictine nun; began writing to Hildegard in the 1150s for encouragement in setting down visions she had concerning URSULA AND THE 11,000 VIRGINS.

EUCHARIST. From the Greek "give thanks"; another name for the MASS of the Faithful; sometimes simply means the presence of Christ in the form of bread.

EUGENIUS III, POPE (FEBRUARY 15, 1145–JULY 8, 1153). Established orthodoxy of Hildegard's visions at the Synod of Trier in the winter of 1147–48.

EXULTET. At the beginning of the Paschal Vigil (see LITURGICAL SEASONS), the community meets in the dark outside the church, a new fire is struck and blessed, a large candle lit, with many individually held candles lit from it. All bear their lights into the church, and the deacon stands before the large flame and sings the Exultet: "Let the angelic heavenly choirs exult. . . . Let earth, too, be joyful, in the radiance of this great splendor." The lengthy, beautiful chant recounts in ecstasy the history of salvation: "O necessary sin of Adam, that Christ's death blotted out! O happy fault, that merited such a Redeemer! O truly blessed night, alone deserving to know the time and hour in which Christ rose from the grave!"

FREDERICK BARBAROSSA, EMPEROR (1121–1190). Crowned king in 1152 and Holy Roman Emperor in 1155. Correspondent of Hildegard.

GLOSSA ORDINARIA. Marginal and interlineary commentaries from the church fathers written in the Bible, added to by medieval theologians such as WALAFRID STRABO, BEDE, and Rabanus Maurus; essentially complete by the twelfth century.

GODFREY. Monk from DISIBODENBERG who began the first VITA or biography of Hildegard.

GREAT SILENCE. Time of strictest monastic silence, inner and exterior, that begins with the OFFICE of Compline in the evening and extends through the end of MASS the next morning; considered to be one of the wellsprings of contemplative life.

GUIBERT. Monk of Gembloux, admirer of Hildegard and correspondent from 1175. Their letters are a primary source for biographical information about Hildegard. He became her secretary and PROVOST at Rupertsberg in 1177 at her request and remained there for a year after her death, at which time he was recalled to Gembloux.

HELENGERUS, ABBOT. Head of the monastery of DISIBODENBERG after KUNO.

HENRY II (1133–1189). King of England and correspondent with Hildegard. He was author of the Constitutions of Clarendon, which codified certain prerogatives regarding royal versus ecclesiastical courts and was opposed by Thomas BECKET.

HOLY INNOCENTS. Children slaughtered by Herod in his attempt to make certain the killing of the child Jesus; their feast is celebrated on December 28, within the OCTAVE of Christmas.

HOLY WEEK, see LITURGICAL SEASONS.

HUGO. Hildegard's brother, cantor at Mainz Cathedral.

HYMN. Nonscriptural poem set to music, popular in its sentiment and rhythm; see OFFICE.

INTERDICT. Religious chastisement imposed by pope or bishop on a person, community, town, or country; usually forbids the regular celebration of or participation in MASS, OFFICE, and sacraments (baptism, confession, etc.).

JUTTA OF SPONHEIM (D. 1136). Of noble birth, Jutta was enclosed as an anchoress at DISIBODENBERG while still a young woman. She became Hildegard's sole caretaker and first teacher when Hildegard was given as OBLATE by her parents in 1106.

KUNO, ABBOT. Head of the monastery at DISIBODENBERG, where Hildegard spent her life from age eight through her mid-forties, at which time she took her small community of women to establish a new monastery at Rupertsberg.

LAWRENCE, ST. (D. 258). Deacon and martyr of Rome whose feast is celebrated on August 10. Legend has it that his punishment for upholding the faith was to be roasted on a gridiron.

LESSON. Liturgical reading from Scriptures, the Church Fathers, or the Lives of the Saints. See OFFICE.

LITURGICAL SEASONS. Extended periods of the year celebrating aspects of the life of Christ and the Church:

Advent. At once the beginning and the ending of the liturgical year, anticipating the coming of Christ into the world at Christmas and his final coming at the end of time (Parousia).

Christmas. Celebration of Christ's birth by Mary on earth—and, by extension, of the Father in eternity.

Epiphany. The manifestation of Christ to the Magi at his birth, as a teacher and worker of wonders, and in glory at the end of time.

Lent. From the Latin "long," a time of penitence; culminates in Holy Week and the Triduum or three days celebrating Christ's passion: Maundy Thursday, Good Friday, and the Paschal Vigil.

Easter. Celebrates Christ's resurrection from death and ascension into heaven.

Pentecost. Celebrates the coming of the Holy Spirit (WISDOM) to the apostles and disciples and the continued work of that Spirit throughout history.

LITURGY. Traditional formal actions performed by or in the name of a religious community. In the Christian Catholic Church the chief liturgical actions are MASS, OFFICE, and the sacraments (the latter referring to specific iconic acts suited to the various stages of life).

MAGDALENE, ST. MARY. One of Christ's disciples, present at his crucifixion, primary witness to his resurrection. She developed a great following in the Middle Ages; many attributes were ascribed to her and myths told about her, and she was the subject of many works of art.

MAGISTRA, MAGISTER. A medieval Latin term of academic rank, still in use today, indicating a person's role as teacher. Correspondents often used this term when addressing Hildegard.

MASS. Liturgical presence and reenactment of the death and glorification of Christ, ending in a communion with Christ in the form of bread and wine. Divided into the Mass of the Catechumens, for those studying the faith, similar in its readings and prayers to the Jewish synagogue service; and the Mass of the Faithful, for baptized initiates.

The proper parts that change according to the feast being celebrated; sung by SCHOLA CANTORUM:

Introit. "Entrance-song"; ANTIPHON sung in PROCESSION, stating the theme of the feast being celebrated.

Gradual. "Step," wherefrom at the altar the cantor originally sang this response to a New Testament reading.

Alleluia. Psalm verse with Alleluias, sung to accompany the procession at the Gospel.

Tract. Ancient, ornate PSALM verses; replaces the Alleluia during times of penance or mourning.

Sequence. A sort of HYMN, popular in nature, whose melody and text move in strophic pairs; occasional use.

Offertory. ANTIPHON sung in PROCESSION accompanying the bringing of bread, wine, and other gifts to the altar; a portion of the antiphon is sung after one to four ornate solo verses. Begins Mass of the Faithful.

Communion. ANTIPHON sung in alternation with psalmody; accompanies the Communion PROCESSION.

The ordinary parts, relatively unchanging, that are sung by the community or the celebrant:

Kyrie eleison. "Lord have mercy. Christ, have mercy. Lord have mercy." Each petition is sung three times.

Gloria in excelsis. Song of praise based on the word of the angels to the shepherds at Christmastide.

Credo. Statement of beliefs; follows the Gospel, ends the Mass of the Catechumens.

Præfatio and *Sanctus.* The celebrant-sung "bridge" connecting the Offertory to the *Canon missæ* or unchanging reenactment of the Mass, immediately followed by the thrice-sung "Holy."

Agnus dei. "Lamb of God," petition for mercy and peace; precedes the reception of Communion.

MISSAL. Altar book containing all the texts and some of the music for the MASS.

NATIVITY OF THE VIRGIN. One of four major Marian feasts in place by Hildegard's day.

OBLATE. From the Latin *oblatus,* from *offere,* "to offer"; denotes a person formally dedicated to a monastery. Scholars still debate the exact meaning the word had when it was used to describe Hildegard's presentation at age eight to JUTTA at DISIBODENBERG.

OCTAVE. Eight-day celebration of a major feast.

OFFICE. Structures of ANTIPHONS, PSALMS, LESSONS, RESPONSORIES, HYMNS, and PRAYERS sung eight "hours" daily; extends the liturgical presence of the MASS.

The Hours of the Office:

Matins. The "morning" hour, correctly sung in the dead of night; it consists of Invitatory, hymn, three Nocturns (each consisting of antiphon and psalms followed by three lessons with their responsories), and the TE DEUM. The Invitatory consists of a recurring antiphon with Ps. VULGATE 94, "Come, let us rejoice unto the Lord, let us shout with joy to the Rock of our salvation!"

Lauds. The dawn "praise," consisting of antiphons and psalms, a hymn, the Canticle of Zachary ("Blessed be the Lord, the God of Israel"), and a prayer.

Prime. "First" of four Little Hours, each having hymn, antiphon with three psalms, and prayers; 6:00 AM.

Terce, sext, and *none.* "Third," "sixth," and "ninth" hours of the day (9:00 AM, noon, 3:00 PM).

Vespers. The "evening" hour, sung at the time of the lighting of the lamps against the dark. As at Lauds, except for the Canticle of Mary, "My soul doth magnify the Lord" (Magnificat).

Compline. The hour of "completion," always the same, in the dark before retiring; begins the GREAT SILENCE.

OFFICE OF THE DEAD. Regular OFFICE structure with specified PSALMS and chants commemorating the dead. Used for ALL SOULS and at the time of an individual's death and at regular memorials.

PASCHAL III, ANTIPOPE. Pretender to the papal throne from April 22, 1164, to September 20, 1168.

PASCHAL VIGIL, see LITURGICAL SEASONS.

PHILIP OF HEINSBERG (D. 1191). A correspondent with Hildegard who testified for her in the lifting of the INTERDICT. He became archbishop of Cologne in 1167.

PORTRESS. A nun who is in charge of caring for the door of the monastery, whose task it therefore is to deal with people in the world outside.

PRAYER. Refers especially to the chief prayer for the day's feast, sometimes called a Collect, used at MASS and in the OFFICE at Lauds, Terce, Sext, None, and Vespers.

PRIORESS. The one who is, after the abbess herself, the "first" in charge in a convent or women's monastery.

PROCESSION. Liturgical movement of celebrant, SCHOLA CANTORUM, and/or congregation, accompanied by song.

PROVOST. For Hildegard, the provost was a monk-priest who was needed to preside regularly at MASS and who would be, in official and ceremonial matters, second only to her in monastic authority.

PSALMS. Old Testament book of 150 songs that are the basis of Catholic LITURGY.

PURIFICATION. In medieval times the Purification, a fixed feast falling on February 2, was considered one of the Marian feasts; its name derives from the ritual practice under Jewish law that took place forty days after childbirth. It celebrates the events recounted in the Gospel of St. Luke (2:31–39) that culminate in the Song of Simeon, in which Christ is "a light to lighten the Gentiles"; hence, the name Candlemas in England and Candelaria in Spanish-speaking countries.

RAINALD OF DASSEL (D. 1167). Made chancellor to FREDERICK BARBAROSSA in 1156 and archbishop of Cologne in 1159.

REQUIEM. Latin for "rest"; regular MASS structure with chants commemorating the dead. Celebrated for ALL SOULS and at the time of an individual's death and at regular memorials.

RESPONSORY. Verses from a psalm sung by the SCHOLA CANTORUM as a commentary to a LESSON in the OFFICE; in the MASS it is called the Gradual. Its form is characterized by a reprise, A-B-A.

RIKKARDA VON STADIS (D. 1152). Young nun at Disibodenberg who, with Volmar, encouraged Hildegard in her first efforts to write down her visions. She was called to be abbess at BASSUM, a promotion probably engineered by her brother Hartwig, who was archbishop of Bremen. Hildegard's efforts to keep her at Rupertsberg were thwarted. Rikkarda died within the year of her move.

RÜDESHEIM, see EIBINGEN.

RULE OF ST. BENEDICT. Rule of monastic behavior set down in the sixth century by Benedict of Nursia. Prescribes in remarkable detail a particularly balanced regimen for life in a community where the singing of the Divine OFFICE is the central work. Stability of residence, obedience, and conversion (from fear to love) are required, and these join the ubiquitous Gospel counsels of poverty and chastity. The prevalent rule for monastic communities from the late eighth century to the present.

RUPERTSBERG. Hildegard named her first convent "Mount Rupert" after St. Rupert of Bingen, wrote a short *vita* to revive the saint's memory, and composed texts and music for a SEQUENCE and three ANTIPHONS to celebrate a LITURGY for him. According to her *vita,* Rupert showed from earliest childhood a great sensitivity to the poor and needy, though he himself was slow in reasoned thought.

He and his noble mother, Bertha, made dwellings and an oratory for the homeless and ministered to them. After Rupert's death at age twenty, a congregation of brothers continued his work; it was on the ruins of their monastery that Hildegard built her own monastery after leaving Disibodenberg. In stressing how the spirit of WISDOM was able to speak through this unschooled, humble young saint who was devoted to the arts of healing and care, it is likely that Hildegard was setting clearcut ideals for her nuns and, as well, making a statement to the world about the purposes of her monastic community.

SANCTORAL CYCLE. The sum of feasts celebrating the lives or martyrdoms of holy persons.

SAPIENTIA, or WISDOM. Female figure in the Bible who "was with God from the beginning" and figures predominantly in the books of Proverbs, Wisdom, and Ecclesiasticus. Throughout Hildegard's visionary works, the Voice of Wisdom consistently interprets her visions, assigning complex meanings to all the colorful details.

SCHOLA CANTORUM. Small group devoted to studying/singing liturgical music, especially the proper or changeable parts of the MASS.

SCIVIAS. "To Know the Ways [of the Lord]." Hildegard's first book of visions, which she dictated to Volmar between 1141 and 1151.

SCRIPTORIUM. Room devoted to the writing of manuscripts, which typically was done through dictation: a reader would read from a book to be copied (perhaps loaned from another monastery), and one or more copyists would produce new books; extra copies made in this way might be exchanged for extra copies produced by other monasteries.

SEQUENCE, see MASS.

STRABO, see WALAFRID STRABO.

SUSANNA. Old Testament figure appearing in chapter 13 of the Book of Daniel, which tells the story of a beautiful young woman named Susanna who was charged with adultery by two lecherous old men. She is vindicated at the end by Daniel's wisdom; the story became in medieval times symbolic of the virtuous soul saved.

SYMMYSTA, see VOLMAR.

TE DEUM. "We praise thee, God," the great hymn of thanksgiving that frequently closes the hour of Matins in the OFFICE. Possibly a compilation of several earlier hymns, its use may be traced to the late fourth century.

TEMPORAL CYCLE. The sum of feasts celebrating the mysteries of Christ's life, divided into LITURGICAL SEASONS.

TRIDUUM, see LITURGICAL SEASONS.

URSULA AND THE 11,000 VIRGINS. Feast celebrated throughout the Western Church on October 21. Ursula's story, known primarily through the many reprintings of *The Golden Legend* of Jacobus Voragine, tells of the life, vision, pilgrimage, and passion (martyrdom) of a Christian princess and her band of virgin followers; we also know it through the inspired paintings of Memling and Carpaccio. The story is based on an ancient Roman inscription in Cologne, which testifies to the fact that a small group of Christian virgins was martyred there, perhaps by marauding Huns, in the fourth century. (The "11,000 virgins" is a scribal error; early in the transmission of the legend, someone mistakenly transcribed the Latin *XI MV* as "*XI mille* [thousand] *virgines*" instead of *"XI martyres virgines"*!) Although the Church was from the first skeptical of Ursula's story and has long since eliminated all of the specific music for the MASS and OFFICE of her feast, her importance in the minds of medieval and Renaissance painters, hagiographers, and believers was beyond mere reason. During Hildegard's lifetime the great zeal for St. Ursula intensified; her story elaborated and spread. In 1106, workmen, enlarging the walls around the city of Cologne, struck what must have been an ancient Roman burial ground right outside the Church of St. Ursula, and the belief was that the bones found there were those of Ursula and her followers. This seemed such powerful physical evidence that the bones were sought by individual parishes and communities throughout Europe and often housed in artistically exquisite reliquaries. The figure of Ursula was undoubtedly Hildegard's most important role model.

URSULA SONGS. Texts and music for use in the OFFICE and MASS written by Hildegard in honor of St. URSULA. Extant are thirteen songs (two RESPONSORIES, one HYMN, one SEQUENCE, and nine ANTIPHONS).

VICTOR IV, ANTIPOPE. Claimant to the papacy from September 7, 1159, to April 20, 1164.

VITA. Latin word meaning "life"; refers in the medieval church to a written biography.

VOICE OF WISDOM, see SAPIENTIA.

VOLMAR (D. 1173). Secretary-scribe to Hildegard from 1141; her magister or teacher and confidant. With great difficulty, Hildegard was able to take Volmar with her when she founded her autonomous community at RUPERTSBERG, where he served as PROVOST until his death. She called him her *symmysta,* or partner in understanding the mysteries.

VULGATE. Translations into Latin from the Old and New Testaments made by St. Jerome in the late fourth century; name given in the sixth century to the then current complete Latin Bible using portions of Jerome's work.

WALAFRID STRABO (CA. 808–849). Student of the great Rabanus Maurus (author of the HYMN *Veni creator spiritus*); monk, theologian, liturgist, and poet. *Hortulus,* on the joys of monastic gardening, is his most famous poem.

WEZELIN. Nephew to Hildegard.

WISDOM. Described as knowledge of the Logos or WORD by which all things are steered through all things. See *SAPIENTIA.*

WORD. Rich concept from the Hebrew and Greek *(logos).* Basically it has reference to what comes from divinity, in the breath: thus it is the offspring of the Father, linked to Him in the Holy Spirit; the Scriptures, as the verbal outpouring of God; the whole cosmos, as the expression of the Father in the creative Spirit-breath; any writing, insofar as it is in-spired with divinity (Ps. VULGATE 44: "My heart hath uttered a good word"). It is also creative knowledge itself, as in verse 15 of Ps. 147: "See how he issues his command to the earth, how swift his word runs!"

Suggested Reading

The bibliography at the end of my first book, *The Journal of Hildegard of Bingen* (New York: Bell Tower, 1993), lists in detail the sources that lie behind the research—especially for music and liturgy—that is a fundament for my understanding of Hildegard. The present book is a reflection on that fundament and the knowledge it has brought me, so there is no formal bibliography. All my translations of Hildegard's exact words are based on the Latin texts found in Hildegard von Bingen, *Patrologia latina,* vol. 197, ed. J. P. Migne (Paris: Palmé, 1855). Critical Latin editions of Hildegard are being published in Turnhout by Corpus Christianorum: Continuatio Mediaevalis (CCCM). Two volumes of letters have appeared, *Epistolarium,* edited by Lieven Van Acker (CCCM 91–91a, 1991, 1993); her book *De operatione dei* appears as *Liber divinorum operum,* edited by Peter Dronke and Albert Derolez (CCCM 92, 1996); her life is given in the *Vita S. Hildegardis,* edited by Monika Klaes (CCCM 126, 1993).

When I began my research more than twenty-five years ago, few sources existed outside the Migne, and there were no English translations. Fortunately, this has changed radically over the past ten years, and now the availability of critical editions of Hildegard's works in Latin as well as in English translation increases with every month. For example, the first volume of a long-awaited English translation of Hildegard's correspondence has been prepared by Joseph L. Baird and Radd K. Ehrman: *The Letters of Hildegard of Bingen,* vol. 1 (New York: Oxford Univ. Press, 1994). The Select Bibliography in Sabina Flanagan's *Secrets of God* (Boston: Shambhala Publications, 1996) is a trusted guide for other sources and translations.

Sabina Flanagan's biography *Hildegard of Bingen: A visionary life* (London: Routledge, 1989) is the best biography we have in English. Flanagan's thought about the meaning of the terms *anchoress* and *oblate* in Hildegard's early life has evolved further and can be found in her essay, "Oblate or Enclosure: Reflections on Hildegard of Bingen's Entry into Religion," in *Wisdom Which Encircles Circles: Papers on Hildegard of Bingen,* ed. Audrey Ekdahl Davidson (Kalamazoo: Medieval Institute Publications, 1996).

Readers interested in the texts of Hildegard's songs will want to read Barbara Newman's *Symphonia* (Ithaca, NY: Cornell Univ. Press, 1988). Newman gives both literal and free translations of each song, plus historical and exegetical information for each. The music for the songs and for Hildegard's sung morality play *Ordo virtutum* is available in standard chant notation in *Hildegard von Bingen: Lieder,* ed. Pudentiana Barth, M. Immaculata Ritscher, and Joseph Schmidt-Görg (Salzburg: Otto Müller, 1969).

Ivan Illich has written a wonderful work—nominally a commentary on the twelfth-century Hugh of St. Victor's *Didascalicon.* It is called *In the Vineyard of the Text* (Chicago: Univ. of Chicago Press, 1993) and embodies Illich's insights into the change in the function of the book from early monasticism, when books were sacred and one read in order to grow, to the era of scholasticism and the university, when one used books as a source of ideas. The time of this transition is exactly congruent with the lifetime of Hildegard, and Illich's thought provides deep insights into the monastic culture of her time. He also helps us understand our own era, in which books lie unread, text begins to disappear, and computer-retrievable and largely disembodied information is an overriding concern.

George H. Putnam's two-volume *Books and Their Makers During the Middle Ages* (1896–97; reprint, NY: Hillary House, 1962) is a fascinating study for those interested in the history of books and medieval scriptoria. It includes solid evidence for the activity of nuns as scribes, even in the early medieval period. The difference between the Latin *dicendo* (speaking or dictating) and *scribendo* (writing) regarding the authorship of medieval texts is nicely clarified.

Books on Thomas Becket abound, not the least of which is T. S. Eliot's play *Murder in the Cathedral.* Scholarly research about the martyr of Canterbury continues; my source for the little song from Becket's period of exile in France is Denis Stevens, "Thomas Becket et la musique medievale," in *Thomas Becket: Actes du Colloque International de Sédières 19–24 Août 1973* (Paris: Editions Beauchesne, 1975), which contains other interesting essays about Becket.